Choc

by Brooke Taylor

Joined by
an ecumenical community of Christian writers

Project Director:	Brooke Taylor
Editor:	Katherine L. Szerdy
Project Coordinators:	Brooke Taylor
	Katherine L. Szerdy
Cover Art:	Ali Towle
Text Design:	Katherine L. Szerdy

Printed and bound in the United States of America.

This book was printed by **Total Printing Systems, Inc.**, 201 South Gregory St., Newton, IL 62448. They can be reached by phone at 866-869-6854, by Fax 618-783-8407, by email at sales@tps1.com, and on the internet at www.tps1.com

ISBN-13: 978-0692976432
ISBN-10: 0692976434

For bulk orders or reorders, please contact www.brooketaylor.us

Books can also be purchased on Amazon or from local booksellers.

Dedication

To my daughter, Karolina...
You remind me to choose joy
every day of my life.

Table of Contents

About the Cover Art

by Ali Towle

When I think about joy, I think about hope. Without hope, without the possibility of something better coming, it is hard to find joy. When designing the cover for this book and while praying about the title *Choose Joy*, the Holy Spirit brought to mind the idea of our Holy Mother as the *New Eve*. While Eve said *yes* to the serpent's lies and brought sin into the world, Mary's *yes* to God at the Annunciation brought salvation, joy, and hope. By painting Mary in the Garden of Eden, it evokes a renewal of the place where sin was first brought into the world. It portrays order where there was once disarray and beauty where there was once sadness.

Because of Mary's *yes* to God, we can all have true joy and unending hope as the child that she bore triumphed over sin and death so that we may have eternal life in heaven with Him. No matter the hardships that we encounter in our lives, we are able to live with the hope that this is not the end. We can look to Mary during these times of tribulation, when the waters are deep, and the world around us seems to be falling apart because Mary herself went through the hardest of times when she witnessed her son's torture and death. We can find comfort in her because we know those horrendous moments were not the end for her either.

Pope Francis once stated, "There are difficult moments in life, but with hope, the soul goes forward and looks ahead to what awaits us." Let us look ahead, Brothers and Sisters, and have the courage to choose the joy that has been won for us.

Introduction

Women need fellowship. I remember visiting my aunt at the nursing home and observing a group of elderly women seated at a table together giggling like schoolgirls. I could almost see them in saddle shoes and pigtails, laughing as little ladies in a different time and place. Introvert or extrovert, old or young, as women, we need one another.

During the early years of motherhood, gatherings may be few and far between. It is a blessed occasion when we get together with other women who understand what it's like to be lonely despite a noisy house and a multitude of duties to keep us busy.

God created women to need community, a circle of friends to encourage, support, love, to lift each other up during the dark times, to rally around and celebrate milestones. As our lives feel more frazzled and fragmented in these tumultuous times, *Choose Joy* was created to help fulfill that need—to expand our circle. Fr. Edward Hays says we are truly "Hobos" meaning "HOmeward BOund." We walk as holy pilgrims on a journey to heaven. What a gift to have the opportunity to stop long enough to meet other Hobos sojourning along the way. Although we cannot always gather in person, sharing our stories in written form can sometimes be just as potent.

One of my most cherished privileges was spending time connecting with listeners as a Christian morning show co-host. Radio has been my career of choice, and while I was fortunate enough to work at top stations in major cities, none was so precious to me as the faith-based contemporary Christian station where I encountered Christ so intimately for over nine years.

I always thought my job there would be my crown and glory. Today, though, instead of 500,000 listeners tuning *in,* I now speak to five beautiful children who tune me *out!* I left my job to be a full-time wife and mom to care for my family, including my special needs daughter. The vocation I have been called to as wife and mother is the supreme joy of my life.

Admittedly, though, the transition has been difficult. I miss the fellowship. I miss connecting with other women from all walks of life and learning from their stories. Through my dad's cancer diagnosis and death, my son's stroke, homeschooling, adoption, a surprise baby and my daughter's diagnosis of autism, the listeners became family despite our different church affiliations and diverse backgrounds. We walked together through the peaks and valleys and learned from each other, as humble Hobos.

Being home with my family has allowed me to answer God's call to women's ministry through starting a weekly podcast called *Good Things Radio*, and organizing an annual retreat called Arise. Both have attracted a growing audience of women from all over the country and all walks of life—women who are seeking encouragement, spiritual growth, and community. It is this community which gave birth to *Choose Joy*.

As I prayed about a title, *Choose Joy* emerged from deep within the DNA of Spirit. I believe it is a summons from our Father to claim the promises of the resurrection--life over death, light over darkness.

The women and men who have lent their voices to this project represent many different Christian traditions. Like a dazzling pallet of colors, fibers and textures, their stories weave a tapestry of witnesses to His love for us. Within these pages you will encounter a Catholic monk (Fr. Nathan Cromly, CSJ) who shares deep insights about suffering and the triumph of the cross. You will meet an African American pastor (Linda Isaiah) who confesses deep generational wounds stemming from slavery and chronic abuse. You will walk alongside a widow (Joan Spieth), rejoice with a military mom (Janie Reinart), learn from a Bible scholar (Jeff Cavins), grieve with a mother who lost her young daughter (Jen Gerber) and embrace the story of an immigrant family and their faith (Katherine Szerdy). This devotional is truly universal in the sense that we focus on what unites us as believers. Each author shares a witness to the power of an authentic living faith.

We have formatted this book to follow the church calendar (Lectionary Year B of the Roman Catholic Church and the Revised

Common Lectionary) beginning with the first Sunday of Advent and ending with Christ the King Sunday. Each week's devotion is based on a designated scripture for that week and is followed by a question for reflection as an invitation to dig deeper. Space has been provided for you to journal your response in words or images.

Jean Vanier said it best: *"Along with the celebration that rises from a community of thanksgiving, there is a note of pain but also a note of hope. We have been drawn together by God to be a sign of resurrection and a sign of unity in this world where there is so much division and inner and outer death. We feel small and weak, but we are gathered together to signify the power of God to transform death into life."*

It is my prayer that this humble work of love will serve as an invitation to immerse ourselves into God's word and respond to our Father's invitation to Choose Joy!

In His love,

Brooke

Hymn to Joy

Joy is prayer
Joy is strength
Joy is love
Joy is a net of love
By which you can catch souls
--Saint Mother Teresa of Calcutta

How to Get the Most from this Book

In order to get the maximum spiritual benefit from this book, we offer the following suggestions:

(1) Grab a cup of tea and....

(2) Try *Lectio Divina*, Latin for "sacred reading," dating back to early monasticism. This practice allows us to let go of our own plans and slowly open ourselves up to encounter the living God. A twelfth century Carthusian monk named Guigo elaborates on this Benedictine practice with four steps:
1. *Reading* seeks
2. *Meditation* finds
3. *Prayer* asks
4. *Contemplation* tastes

First, **read** the Bible passage aloud, perhaps more than once, each time allowing silence for a minute afterward for **meditation** on the reading. Next, **pray** the scriptures—how can you turn the reading into a prayer? And finally, the reflection questions, each carefully written to elicit a deep, soulful **contemplation**, are provided at the end of each devotion along with room for you to write. We encourage you to take the time to not just ruminate about the questions, but to prayerfully invite the Holy Spirit to use your pen [or colored pencils, watercolors, Crayola markers] to uncover, reveal, inspire, surprise you with an insight, a discernment, wisdom. We have found that when we attend to the message in this way, there is a deep spiritual nourishment. God can use this exercise to teach us something more, to show us how to choose joy.

(3) Gather with a group. Consider starting a *Choose Joy* study. The weekly format allows for manageable readings. The reflection questions may be used individually or in a larger setting.

Jesus said to his disciples: "Be watchful! Be alert!" (Mark 13:33-37 NAB)

Lessons from a Summer Bike Ride
by Anna Bertram

This past summer my daughter, Molly, enjoyed riding her bike as I walk around the neighborhood. As usual, she was a bit ahead of me. During these walks, I usually talk to God. I tell Him my hopes for the future and the fears that are holding me back; I ask for guidance and to remain in His Will.

This particular day, I was pleading with Him for grace, pouring my heart out hoping that He would fill it back up. As we stopped to cross the street, we looked both ways and safely crossed. As Molly peddled off ahead of me, the thought came to mind, "I really need to tell her to stop at that house before she crosses the driveway." She was already approaching the driveway.

Just then I saw a car backing out directly in line with Molly. Flailing my arms trying to get the drivers attention, I screamed, "STOP! She is behind you!" I offered up a quick "God please help!"

Upon hearing my cry for help, Molly quickly jumped off the bike and started running towards me. The car stopped with only inches to spare. Molly was sobbing and I was a mommy mess. I wanted to yell at the woman behind the wheel and react in anger towards her. Did she even look behind her? My anger quickly turned to a paralyzing fear as I was in shock thinking what almost happened. I was quickly jolted back to reality as the driver of the car rolled down her window and apologized for scaring my daughter. I asked if she had seen her. She told me "No."

As I retrieved Molly's bike from behind her car, I comforted her, still very upset and shaken. I asked God to guide my words to her. "Everything will be ok. You did the right thing by jumping off your bike and running to me." Grace washed over me as I asked her, "What made you think to do that?"

Her little voice squeaked as she responded, "Something in my head told me to." I explained that the little voice she heard was God and her Guardian Angel was watching over her. She looked up at me and smiled. We gave thanks to God for watching over us and keeping us safe from harm and thanked her guardian angel for looking after her. We continued the rest of the way and made it safely home.

In today's gospel, Jesus tells his disciples, "Be watchful! Be alert!" It is easy to get caught up in the stresses and busy-ness of everyday life. Consumed at times with our own selfish desires, we forget that we need to make room for God in our day, to take time to listen. I could have lashed out at the woman in front of my daughter. Instead, I believe God was telling me to be alert. It is a lesson that I will not soon forget. Just as Molly jumped off her bike into my arms, our loving Father is waiting for us to jump into His, without hesitation. Our children teach us so very much. He waits for us to wake up from our sleep to sit with Him, to run toward Him, to abide in Him. For in Him our soul finds rest.

Reflection: During this Advent season, how can you be more watchful and alert of His grace guiding you? What lesson is He waiting to teach you? Will you let Him speak to your heart? Will you be like the gatekeeper and be watchful? Or will He find you sleeping?

John was clothed in camel's hair, with a leather belt around his waist. He fed on locusts and wild honey. And this is what he proclaimed: "One mightier than I is coming after me. I am not worthy to stoop and loosen the thongs of his sandals." (Mark 1: 6-7 NAB)

What Matters Most
by Brooke Taylor

This passage pulls me back to the true simplicity of Christmas. John, clothed only in camel's hair and a crude leather belt, spends his days in the desert. It is in this environment a prophet is free to hear God. John confidently echoes the words of Isaiah to proclaim the Lord's coming.

The sand, sweat, dung and locusts are a far cry from the glittery greens and reds, synthetic images, shopping lists, and digital devices of our day. This is a radical reversal of the Incarnation--the Source of all love and liberation, the God of the Universe, coming to us in utter poverty.

On May 29, 2011, we picked up our daughter from an orphanage in Czestochowa, Poland. As I held her, we were given a small paper bag. Inside contained a crib sheet, a blanket, two baby bottles, and a pillow. This was the sum total of our eleven-month-old daughter's earthly belongings. While her material possessions may have been scarce, our love was greater than anything the world could ever provide. We believed that the treasure we held in our arms was beyond price. It was a powerful reminder that the "stuff" I often place value in, is of little value at all.

Our journey to Karolina reminds me that toys are not the same as *gifts*. No amount of money can buy

Forgiveness
  Wisdom
    Love
      Contentment
        Time
          Salvation.

Like modern day Magi, we are called to bypass Best Buy for Bethlehem. We may bring our gifts along the way, but our journey continues until we reach the place of the nativity. In a world bloated by superfluous stuff, I embrace the simplicity of that moment in the orphanage. Having nothing, we received everything...the Gift of Life.

That singular moment taught me never to be afraid. When everything else is stripped away, we are free to hear Our Lord. It is the same salutation that the angels proclaimed to the shepherds in the field. "Do not be afraid!" We left the orphanage knowing that Emmanuel--God With Us--was more real than the ground we stand on. In our lack, our fear and in our love, He is there.

It takes courage to be a follower of Christ. Today, the world of John the Baptist seems so alien. I imagine him standing in line at the big box store with camel hair tunic and vacuum-packed locusts telling the shoppers "One mightier than I is coming!" How quickly would he become an object of viral vitriol? In his time, John was greatly respected. Many thought he was the Messiah. His words are just as true today. His voice echoes through the centuries into our time and specifically into our lives of plenty to call us "out" to join him.

Like the shepherds in the field, we have been chosen to receive "Good news of great joy!" We are called to demonstrate that the most important gifts are those freely given: mercy, prayer, thanksgiving, acts of service, and a faith that speaks to the world of what really matters. Even a smile is a gift!

St. Paul tells us that we are "co-heirs, members of the same body, and co-partners in the promise of Christ Jesus. (Eph.3:6). What greater gift can we ask for, than the nobility that comes with being an adopted child of God!

Reflection: Recall a time when you felt the presence of God during a time of lack. How did he provide for you? On a separate sheet of paper, draw a picture of His provision and post that picture in a conspicuous place as a remembrance of His grace throughout the week.

Brothers and sisters:
Rejoice always. Pray without ceasing.
In all circumstances give thanks,
for this is the will of God for you in Christ Jesus.
Do not quench the Spirit.
Do not despise prophetic utterances.
Test everything; retain what is good.
Refrain from every kind of evil.

May the God of peace make you perfectly holy
and may you entirely, spirit, soul, and body,
be preserved blameless for the coming of our Lord Jesus Christ.
The one who calls you is faithful,
and he will also accomplish it. (1 Thessalonians 5:16-24 NAB)

The Source of our Joy
by Marie Monsour

This Sunday is Gaudete Sunday. Gaudete (pronounced "Gaw-DET-tay) is a Latin command meaning, "Be joyful!" The devotional journal you are holding incites you to *Choose Joy!* But what is joy? I know I am not *always* happy. How can I always be joyful?

Theologian Henri Nouwen describes the difference:

While happiness is dependent on external circumstances, joy is
"the experience of knowing that you are unconditionally loved
and that nothing -- sickness, failure, emotional distress,
oppression, war, or even death -- can take that love away."
Therefore, we can have joy even in the midst of sadness and
suffering.

I've seen friends suffer the death of their young child.
I've seen friends suffer all the indignities of cancer and finally succumb to its biting claws.
I've seen friends suffer as their teen and adult children leave the faith behind for the wiles of the world.

I've seen friends suffer from diseases that cause daily pain and struggle.
I've seen friends suffer from mental sicknesses and depression.
I've seen friends suffer from relationships gone bad – divorce, abuse,
infidelity.

And I've stood in awe of those who have chosen joy in the midst of
these great sorrows. I don't know if I understand the secret to choosing
joy in the face of excruciating pain or difficulty. But one thing I know.
God is the *source of joy (Psalm 43:4)*. When faced with trial or
tribulation, we run to God. We run to the source. And there we find
solace. There we will find the strength and the abiding joy that comes
from living in the palm of His hand.

You have turned my mourning into dancing;
you have taken off my sackcloth and clothed me with joy,
so that my soul may praise you and not be silent.
O Lord my God I will give thanks to you forever. (Psalm 30:11-12 NAB)

Reflection: Make this week's scripture your own:
Brothers and sisters:
Rejoice always. Pray without ceasing.
In all circumstances give thanks,
List specific circumstances from this day for which you can give thanks:

    1. _____
    2. _____
    3. _____
    4. _____
    5. _____

4th Sunday in Advent/Christmas

In the sixth month the angel Gabriel was sent from God to a city of Galilee named Nazareth, to a virgin betrothed to a man whose name was Joseph, of the house of David; and the virgin's name was Mary. And he came to her and said, "Hail, O favored one, the Lord is with you!"

But she was greatly troubled at the saying, and considered in her mind what sort of greeting this might be.

And the angel said to her, "Do not be afraid, Mary, for you have found favor with God. And behold, you will conceive in your womb and bear a son, and you shall call his name Jesus. He will be great, and will be called the Son of the Most High; and the Lord God will give to him the throne of his father David, and he will reign over the house of Jacob for ever; and of his kingdom there will be no end."

And Mary said to the angel, "How shall this be, since I have no husband?"

And the angel said to her, "The Holy Spirit will come upon you, and the power of the Most High will overshadow you; therefore the child to be born will be called holy, the Son of God. And behold, your kinswoman Elizabeth in her old age has also conceived a son; and this is the sixth month with her who was called barren. For with God nothing will be impossible."

And Mary said, "Behold, I am the handmaid of the Lord; let it be to me according to your word." And the angel departed from her. (Luke 1:26-38 RSV-CE)

The Gift of *Fiat*
by Fr. Nathan Cromly

What do you do when God does not give you blueprints for your life? What if you are faced with two good things, and have to choose between them? Through the Annunciation story, our Christmas reading offers us a glimpse into Mary as archetype of holy decision-making. Mary teaches us how to know what God wants for us!

The prologue to the Annunciation is Mary's relationship with God, which the angel acknowledges by saying, "the Lord is with you!" For us, the best first step in decision-making is to turn to our relationship with God, praying to Him in surrender. Using our own words, or drawing on the words of others, we can ask for our heart to be inclined to know His will. Blessed Charles de Foucauld's simple yet eminently effective prayer of abandonment begins: "Father, I abandon myself into your hands; do with me what you will. Whatever you may do, I thank you: I am ready for all, I accept all." Pray for abandonment to God's will, even if you don't feel "ready for all"!

Next, learn to use the gift of your mind without fear. The mind is God's creation… let it serve Him! Mary listens not only with her heart but also her mind, and questions the angel, "How can this be?" She inquires so as to better understand what God wants her to do; but, unlike Zechariah, she does not let her inquiry hold her back from acting in trust. If you have thought your decision through and taken the time to seek advice from the wise people in your life, why should you doubt yourself? God likes to hide behind His creatures; often enough, He will speak His will through the truths that our minds detect!

Sometimes the weight of choices seems overwhelming. C.S. Lewis described this world as the "vale of soul-making" because our daily decisions build up momentous consequences for the soul. Yet, in the silence, and despite the gravity of the angel's message, Mary still dares to make a choice. "Behold, I am the handmaid of the Lord," she says, committing herself wholeheartedly to the mission she does not fully understand. From her example, we draw the lesson that decisions can be made—in fact must be made—without perfect certainty. Once you give your *fiat* or yes, commit to it. Give it your all and do not look back! Ships were not made for the harbor, but for the open seas. We were not made for indecision but for bold deeds!

Of course, as you act upon your choice, be humble enough to let God correct your course, be it through circumstances or direct intervention. Just like a GPS, God can "recalculate" our route! But it is better to begin the journey than stand trapped in indecision.

God involved the gift of Mary's "yes" as a beautiful part of the salvific design of history! Let's not wait for New Year's Day to face the resolutions and choices we need to make in our lives. Like Mary, move forward boldly in trust today, knowing that He chose to be born in a manger for you, and you must choose your response.

Reflection: What decisions face me today, this week, this year? How can I surrender them to Him and move forward in trust? Write a prayer of surrender. Using a calligraphy pen or colorful marker, copy that prayer of surrender on a separate piece of paper or cardstock. Place it where you can be reminded of your need for Him.

Now there was a man in Jerusalem, whose name was Simeon, and this man was righteous and devout, looking for the consolation of Israel, and the Holy Spirit was upon him. And it had been revealed to him by the Holy Spirit that he should not see death before he had seen the Lord's Christ. And inspired by the Spirit he came into the temple; and when the parents brought in the child Jesus, to do for him according to the custom of the law, he took him up in his arms and blessed God and said, "Lord, now lettest thou thy servant depart in peace, according to thy word; for mine eyes have seen thy salvation which thou hast prepared in the presence of all peoples, a light for revelation to the Gentiles, and for glory to thy people Israel."

And his father and his mother marveled at what was said about him; and Simeon blessed them and said to Mary his mother, "Behold, this child is set for the fall and rising of many in Israel, and for a sign that is spoken against (and a sword will pierce through your own soul also), that thoughts out of many hearts may be revealed.
(Luke 2:25-35 RSV)

My Simeon
by Katherine L. Szerdy

When I hear this story about Simeon and the Holy Family, I can't help but think about my husband's father. At the age of twelve, my father-in-law Steve Szerdy, Jr., his 14-year-old sister Grace and father Steve Szerdy, Sr., arrived in the tiny village of Fairport Harbor, Ohio, from Hungary via Ellis Island sometime around 1930. When I first heard the story of my father-in-law's immigration, I was shocked to hear that, for reasons unknown to us, they left their mother and wife behind in the "old country" for the promise of a new life in America. Whatever the reason, I wonder if these two young adolescents knew as they waved goodbye that they would never see their mother again. Like many school age non-English speaking immigrants at the time, Steve was placed in second grade because of his inability to speak English. He had to quit school early to get a job when his father's new wife kicked the kids out. His childhood was far from easy.

Three decades later, I came to know my husband's father as a quiet, soft-spoken man of few words. When he spoke, with a remnant of a Hungarian accent, we listened. His words held weight. He and my mother-in-law had a wonderful marriage of 36 years and raised four beautiful children. When my mother-in-law passed away suddenly of a heart attack, I could visibly see his heart break. Though his children tried very hard to encourage him and lift his spirits, we could not interest him in hobbies or family gatherings. His appetite continued to wane and his health began to decline.

The last time I saw Dad was the day I was released from the hospital after giving birth to our first child. He sat down on the couch as I laid our newborn son in his arms. Eyes brimming with tears, he drew my swaddled son close. "Thank you for my grandson," he whispered.

I imagine that Simeon had the same look in his eyes, heart overflowing with gratitude, when he first beheld the Christ child. We don't know much about Simeon as this is his only appearance in the narrative. We don't know from the deep lines in his face about the hardships in his life—nor how the Holy Spirit helped him to overcome life's challenges. But we know enough. Luke tells us he had an intimate relationship with the Holy Spirit. From the text we recognize him as righteous, devout, faithful. He blesses God for the gift, the fulfillment of a promise, to behold the salvation of the Jews and Gentiles. Like my father-in-law, he was at the end of his life. Holding this bundle of hope was the fulfillment of the Holy Spirit's promise to see the light of salvation.

Reflection: When have you or someone you know beheld a sign of our salvation? As a way of honoring that sign, draw or paint a picture of it here.

Blessed be the God and Father of our Lord Jesus Christ, who has blessed us in Christ with every spiritual blessing in the heavenly places, even as he chose us in him before the foundation of the world, that we should be holy and blameless before him. He destined us in love to be his sons through Jesus Christ, according to the purpose of his will, to the praise of his glorious grace which he freely bestowed on us in the Beloved. (Ephesians 1:3-6 RSV-CE)

The Unholy Light in the Darkness
by Melody Lyons

I sat in the dark room with my feverish toddler sleeping restlessly in my arms and my iPad on my knee. The device was dark and dumb, a useless brick. Its battery depleted, it had shut down abruptly into blackness. And I? I was stuck in the silence with a growing frustration. I tried to think of ways that I could set down my child without waking her to go plug in my device and felt a strong prick of irritation when she whimpered.

As I sat in the dark silence, I was alarmed by my lack of compassion for my daughter; and I was startled by my urgent pull toward that iPad. Attempts to pray were met by a mind full of white noise and scattered ideas and images... and that persistent desire to be reconnected to the bright buzzing world hidden behind that mocking black screen. I was startled. *What have I become?*

There was a time in my motherhood when my days were full of silence and my nights were dark. I didn't have a shining device. We didn't have a TV. There were no ear buds attached to my head. Instead, it was hours of quiet with an occasional whispered lullaby. My mind and soul were raw, unrefined versions of my more mature self. I like to believe that I've improved over time, but there was something simple and beautiful about those first years. There was a Christ-peace that the stillness brought and that I never quite recovered.

After my daughter finally fell into a deep sleep, I went to bed and tried to return, not to the empty prayer that I'd fallen into, but the deep prayer of the soul that seeks intimacy with the person of Christ. Several hours later, as the sunrise peeked over the trees, I finally fell asleep... overcome by the mental and emotional fatigue of the effort... and the sorrow of failure.

I was seeking silence and connection; but the hard truth is that I could not shut off the noise in my head. All I wanted now was to go back. *I want to be near to You, Jesus. I want to rest in Your Sacred Heart, place my head on Your holy chest, and hear nothing but the beating of Your very life in my soul.*

That prayer was the beginning of a turning away from attachment to that unholy light in the darkness. God heard my plea and answered with abundant grace to restore the connection which seemed lost. What I saw as a failure in the night was really a holy battle for Love, prompted by His call through grace, and ending in His triumph through my weakness. I was a child stumbling through the dark seeking the hand of my Father... and in the light of the dawn, I saw that He had been with me all along.

Reflection: What things in your life have become obstacles to God's purpose for your soul? What is one distraction you can set aside out of love for Christ today?

You will go on from there until you come to the sacred tree at Tabor, where you will meet three men on their way to offer a sacrifice to God at Bethel. One of them will be leading three young goats, another one will be carrying three loaves of bread, and the third one will have a leather bag full of wine. They will greet you and offer you two of the loaves, which you are to accept. Then you will go to the Hill of God in Gibeah, where there is a Philistine camp. At the entrance to the town you will meet a group of prophets coming down from the altar on the hill, playing harps, drums, flutes, and lyres. They will be dancing and shouting.

Suddenly the spirit of the Lord will take control of you, and you will join in their religious dancing and shouting and will become a different person. When these things happen, do whatever God leads you to do. You will go ahead of me to Gilgal, where I will meet you and offer burnt sacrifices and fellowship sacrifices. Wait there seven days until I come and tell you what to do."

When Saul turned to leave Samuel, God gave Saul a new nature. And everything Samuel had told him happened that day. When Saul and his servant arrived at Gibeah, a group of prophets met him. Suddenly the spirit of God took control of him, and he joined in their ecstatic dancing and shouting. (1 Sam 3: 3-10 Good News Translation-Catholic ed.)

Speak, Lord, Your Servant Is Listening
by Jenni Ellis

At six years of age, I stood in the middle of our family room and told my mother, "When I grow up, I am going to be a teacher." My mother, thinking this was just another idea in a litany of ambitions, said, "That's nice, Jenni. Why do you want to be a teacher?" I knew exactly why and clearly stated, "Because I know I can do a better job than the lady I've got now."

The decision was made. At six, I was called to teach, albeit I may have been a bit inappropriately precocious about it.

From age 21 to 42, I was in what my grandmother calls "the school business." I taught middle school. I was a high school librarian. I was

27

an administrator. Yes, there were some difficult years, but overall I loved it.

That was until the last couple of years. My responsibilities continued to increase and the issues that I had to deal with on a day-to-day basis became insurmountable. The school business was having a negative impact on my relationship with my son and my own personal health.

After 21 years, I decided it was time to leave education altogether. I didn't know what God had in store for me, but I knew it was time for something different. I knew God would reveal His plan for me in time, but what I did know—I was certain that I wasn't going back into education – at least not any time soon.

August arrived. Teachers began going back to school, and the students followed. I wasn't a part of it, and I was miserable. The only days in which I found solace were the ones that former colleagues called me for insight or advice. But, no, I wasn't ready to be back in a school. I was not going back into education. I was supposed to be taking some time off, but having worked since age sixteen, I found I missed working terribly.

The last Sunday night in August I started to look for jobs – in the non-profit sector, not education. That night I wrote in my prayer journal, "Lord, if I am supposed to be working, you are going to need to drop a job into my lap." In a way that was a lot more demanding than Samuel, I said, "Speak, Lord, your servant is listening" (1 Samuel 3:9). I closed my prayer journal and went to sleep.

The next morning, on a whim, I started searching for jobs in education. I knew most schools had already started and the likelihood of any jobs being open was slim to none. But I looked anyway. Even as I pulled up the website, I told myself how ridiculous and what a waste of time it was that I was even looking.

And then there it was. A posting that had been placed earlier in the month for a position in a school that seemed to be made for me. It was position that was being kept open until they could find the right person. I had to get out of my own way and quit trying to control what would and would not happen. I turned it completely over to Him and He gently guided me back to exactly where I needed to be.

Reflection: When you get out of your own way and listen for God, what is He saying?

After John was put in prison, Jesus went into Galilee, proclaiming the good news of God. "The time has come," he said. "The kingdom of God has come near. Repent and believe the good news!" As Jesus walked beside the Sea of Galilee, he saw Simon and his brother Andrew casting a net into the lake, for they were fishermen. "Come, follow me," Jesus said, "and I will send you out to fish for people." At once they left their nets and followed him.

When he had gone a little farther, he saw James son of Zebedee and his brother John in a boat, preparing their nets. Without delay he called them, and they left their father Zebedee in the boat with the hired men and followed him. (Mark 1:14-20 NIV)

An Invitation to Joy
by Rachel G. Scott

Have you ever pursued happiness over joy?

If you have, you are not alone. Not long ago, I was offered a full-time position teaching high school. I was extremely excited about this opportunity because becoming a teacher was my childhood dream. When I was a teenager, I took the time to plan out my life until the age of 30. Why 30? Because as a teenager, 30-years-old feels ancient! So my dream of getting married, owning a home, starting a business, traveling and becoming a full-time teacher were all reasonable things to accomplish by that age. Having children wasn't on my radar at the time.

By 30, I had accomplished most of the things on my list except becoming a full-time teacher. So when I was offered the opportunity to teach full-time, I knew it was destiny.

I went in for the interview over the summer, and though confident that I would be offered the job, I had an overwhelming feeling of discontentment throughout the entire process. I knew that I wasn't supposed to accept the position, but despite my inner turmoil, when it was offered to me, I accepted!

Nothing drastic changed overnight, but over time, I began to notice changes in my business production, family intimacy and overall joy throughout the day. When I finally realized things had changed, I began to pray and ask God why? As I prayed with an open heart and ears, I prepared myself for harsh correction from an angry God because of my apparent disobedience. But instead, I received an invitation from a loving Father that calmly said, *"Come follow me, and I will make you…"*

It was then that God reminded me that accomplishing my will, and not His, would not only deplete me of peace but exclude me from experiencing joy. It is only when I choose to submit my will to Him that I can experience joy because unlike happiness, joy is relational, not situational.

In today's passage, we see four men who understand this concept. Simon, Andrew, James, and John accepted the invitation to "come." They could have stayed in their positions of social acceptance, financial gain and professional status. But instead, they chose to accept the invitation from Jesus when he said, *"Come Follow Me."* These men didn't have all the details of what was to come, but they understood that they had completed their assignment to be fishermen that caught only fish. Fishing for fish was only a means to an end--it was their training ground in how to fish for men, and that's where they would find joy. So they decided to trust the plan of the Master above their own, accept the invitation and experience joy in pleasing God and so can you!

Reflection: In what area do you feel God is inviting you and saying, "Come follow me and I will make you…" and what can you do to trust him in the unknowns of the invitation?

4th Sunday in Ordinary Time (Sunday between January 28 and February 3)

And they went into Caper'na-um; and immediately on the Sabbath he entered the synagogue and taught. And they were astonished at his teaching, for he taught them as one who had authority, and not as the scribes. And immediately there was in their synagogue a man with an unclean spirit; and he cried out, "What have you to do with us, Jesus of Nazareth? Have you come to destroy us? I know who you are, the Holy One of God." But Jesus rebuked him, saying, "Be silent, and come out of him!" And the unclean spirit, convulsing him and crying with a loud voice, came out of him. And they were all amazed, so that they questioned among themselves, saying, "What is this? A new teaching! With authority he commands even the unclean spirits, and they obey him." And at once his fame spread everywhere throughout all the surrounding region of Galilee. (Mark 1:21-28 RSV)

The Astonishment Response
by Katherine L. Szerdy

We read in Mark 1 that those who heard Jesus teach in the synagogue were *astonished* at his teaching. The verb *astonish* indicates a response that is beyond the norm—*astound, stagger, stun* and *confound* are just a few of the synonyms I found in the thesaurus. Mark does not tell us exactly what the Lord was teaching that day, but he does tell us how Jesus taught—as one "who had authority" and "not as the scribes." Where does that sense of astonishment come from? What about Jesus' teaching caused this astonishment response?

As a writer, I often feel that what I have written could not possibly have come out of my brain—that the inspiration or insight came not from me but the Holy Spirit! It's not a heady experience by any means, but a humbling synchronicity that spontaneously erupts from the depths of my soul, and never fails to astonish!

It even happened while I was writing one of the devotions in this book, and the insight that emerged was a cathartic Aha!, one which had never occurred to me nor could anyone ever convince me that such inspiration could possibly have come from the five pounds of gray matter in my head! No, this was God breaking through. And these moments only occur when I am obedient to the discipline of journaling daily as a part of my daily devotional practice.

I write these words as an encouragement to you, dear Reader, to take up the daily practice of keeping a spiritual journal whether it be in the form of daily letters to God, recorded answers to prayer, or a Mass or sermon notebook. You can also use the reflection questions at the end of each devotion in this book to help get you started with a daily journaling discipline. I guarantee it won't be long before the Holy Spirit astonishes you with a breakthrough Aha! moment of your own!

Reflection: When was the last time you were *astonished* by a teaching of the Lord, either in the form of a homily or sermon, Bible study teaching, podcast or conference speaker? Do you remember exactly what was said or was it the conviction with which the teaching was delivered that remains with you still? Have you ever been astonished by an insight that emerged during prayer, journaling, or Bible study?

5th Sunday in Ordinary Time (Sunday between February 4 and 10)

And immediately he left the synagogue, and entered the house of Simon and Andrew, with James and John. Now Simon's mother-in-law lay sick with a fever, and immediately they told him of her. And he came and took her by the hand and lifted her up, and the fever left her; and she served them. (Mark 1:29-31 RSV)

Choosing to Serve Joyfully
by Lisa M. Hendey

After many months of anticipation, I recently experienced the great joy of becoming a "mother-in-law." Admittedly, for too many years the words "mother-in-law" and "joy" were not adjoined in my mind. My vantage point as daughter-in-law gave me a different perspective: one of duty, honor, and responsibility. I wanted my mother-in-law to like me, but I also wanted to do things my own way. Too often, I balked at my husband's mom's wisdom, listening patiently and then opting for a different course.

Now that the tables are turned, I'm praying daily for the grace to fulfill my new station in life with patience, love and joy. So far, I've cut my teeth on simple tasks such as arranging the seating for wedding reception tables or affirming the newlyweds' decision to adopt a puppy. I'm learning to offer my opinions with respect, but also to do more praying than advising. The new woman in my son's life makes this easy. She is a lovely soul who cares so deeply for his physical and spiritual well-being that it's easy to see God's hand in drawing the two of them together.

For many years, I read the early verses of Mark's first chapter without recognizing how Simon's mother-in-law leapt from her sick bed and immediately set about serving. My new role helps me to understand more deeply that her serving—the food she likely prepared, the table she set, the extras she offered—were her way of giving thanks for the miracle bestowed upon her. She who could have chosen to linger in her recuperation instead chose service in the way she knew best. In doing so,

I'm sure her mother-in-law's heart glowed to see Simon with this new Teacher, perhaps savoring her favorite recipes.

Choosing joy sometimes means overcoming the obstacles in life which would hold us back from fully giving ourselves to God and to those around us. It means fighting through fatigue, realizing that most often we will serve quietly and with little recognition. Choosing joy means embracing the path spelled out for us by a Doctor of the Church who in her own day served without spotlight:

"Miss no single opportunity of making some small sacrifice," shares St. Therese of Lisieux, *"here by a smiling look, there by a kindly word; always doing the smallest right and doing it all for love."*

Reflection: What are some simple ways that you can serve those around you without drawing attention to your actions or expecting recognition? How can you adjust your attitude to offer these acts with greater love so that the actions themselves become joyful rewards?

6th Sunday in Ordinary Time (Sunday between February 11 and 17)

So whether you eat or drink, or whatever you do, do everything for the glory of God. Avoid giving offense, whether to Jews or Greeks or the church of God. Just as I try to please everyone in every way, not seeking my own benefit but that of the many, that they may be saved. Be imitators of me, as I am of Christ. (1 Corinthians 10:31-11:1 NAB)

Finding my Calling
by Vicki Przybylski

I have been blessed over the last 30 years to have had many different job titles: waitress, prep cook, fundraiser, security guard, nurse, coach, Girl Scout leader, and Police Officer. However, the most challenging and rewarding job I have had is being a Police Officer. I have been on the job for twelve years.

At the beginning of my career, I was so excited and grateful for the job that I did not allow others' opinions or judgments to phase me. As time passed, the public perception of my job dramatically changed and morale in the department was very low. By 2016, it was so low that I was ashamed of my job. I would not tell people what my job was when asked. If they persisted, I would drop my head and mumble "I'm a cop."

Then, a miraculous thing happened! My dear friends and sisters-in-Christ on the Arise Retreat team gave me a different perspective--that being a Police Officer was not just my job. They helped me to see that, instead, it is a calling...my calling. On the front lines, I can be the hands and feet of Christ to the marginalized of society. In this position, I have the ability to bring people Christ's hope, compassion and love. It was an amazing concept that I clung to on the worst days and rested in on the easier days.

Now, I look at each call for service as a challenge to not just help someone temporarily, but also, to find a way to introduce him or her to Christ or help deepen their faith. The lesson I have learned from this experience is that everyone has a calling and that our calling is an important part of His plan.

Reflection: Do you know what your calling is? How are you using that calling to be Christ to others? If you don't know what your calling is, try asking God to reveal it to you.

"Yet even now," says the Lord, "return to me with all your heart, with fasting, with weeping, and with mourning; and rend your hearts and not your garments." Return to the Lord, your God, for he is gracious and merciful, slow to anger, and abounding in steadfast love…" (Joel 2:12-18 RSV)

What Should I Give Up This Year?
by Katherine L. Szerdy

In this age of gluttonous consumerism, immediate gratification and self-entitlement, fasting is not too popular. We fast to lose weight or increase longevity. Political activists fast to get their point across. But fasting as a spiritual discipline is too much like work despite the fact that we have plenty of role models throughout the Bible to show us how and why it's done. Search the scriptures and you will find nearly all the spiritual heavyweights in the Old Testament practiced fasting—Moses, Hannah, Elijah, Nehemiah and Daniel to name a few. Jesus fasted, and so did Paul at the point of his conversion. In the Sermon on the Mount, Jesus said, "*When* you fast," not "*If* you fast."

In an article entitled "Fasting: Twentieth Century Style," Richard Foster, Pastor, founder of Renovare, an ecumenical ministry, and author of the classic 20th century bestseller *Celebration of Discipline*, describes fasting in this way: "That's it! Learning to disown ourselves. That frees us from the tyranny of our own needs. It frees us from the tyranny of others. It frees us from the tyranny of a proper image. It frees us to have that genuine, God-given self-esteem." Fasting encourages us, as Francis Fenelon, a 17th century Archbishop, said, "to consider God more often than we consider ourselves." And in looking to Him, we are transformed.

I converted to Catholicism this past Easter in part because of my love for the sacraments and spiritual disciplines. Even as a child baptized and confirmed in the Congregational Church, I would fast during Lent and spend extra time studying the scriptures. Something in me just needed to do that; yet, I had no role models, no friends or family who practiced a liturgical faith.

My practice of fasting morphed through the years from giving up chocolate or a meal a day to giving up of my time and treasures. One year, I daily sacrificed the extra time needed to write a card or letter to church shut-ins; another year, I decided to perform a good deed secretly for a loved one or stranger. Last year, I searched my closet each of the 40 days of Lent for one thing to donate to the Salvation Army. During the past few years, I have made it a practice to give up social media for Holy Week. Whatever I choose to sacrifice—time, treasures, treats, or Tweets, I always look forward to Lent as a time to step back from the busy-ness of life to invest more time in my relationship with Jesus, to study His Word, to deeply listen and obey.

Reflection: What Lenten practice has meant the most to you? In addition to whatever Lenten practice your faith tradition encourages, this year, try practicing a daily discipline that might even be a bit of a stretch for you. You might try subscribing to a daily Lenten devotional such as Matthew Kelly's www.dynamiccatholic.com (Click "Sign Up" and subscribe to the free Lenten online devotional sent to your email each day.) Or try spending ten or fifteen minutes in a quiet place at the feet of Jesus. Light a candle to remind you of His ever-presence. Start with prayer and scripture reading. Quiet your heart, relax into His presence and listen deeply. Then journal about what you heard from your heavenly Father.

The Spirit drove Jesus out into the desert, and he remained in the desert for forty days, tempted by Satan. He was among wild beasts, and the angels ministered to him. After John had been arrested, Jesus came to Galilee proclaiming the gospel of God: "This is the time of fulfillment. The kingdom of God is at hand. Repent, and believe in the gospel." (Mark 1: 12-15 NABRE)

Let God Be In Control
by Tanya Weitzel

I spent many years spiritually hiding from God in a desert. I let other people control who I was while Satan tempted me to become a false image of myself. He used my low self-esteem against me. I was weak inside and lacked faith in God, and I allowed Satan to overpower me.

The negative voices in my head were not my own, but Satan's. For many years, I convinced myself I wasn't good enough, smart enough, or perfect enough. Enough for whom? Satan, myself, or God? I was no longer sure where these insecurities came from. I prayed to God to show me how I was harming myself and why I felt like I was dying inside.

In order to draw closer to God, I had to let go of my need for control. It was in that moment that I saw how much I needed God. Satan lied to me. I was never going to be enough in his eyes. God already made me exactly the way I needed to be for Him, my family, my friends, and myself.

Reflection: In what ways have you hid from God? What negative voices play in your head? Try jotting those negative thoughts down to better see them for what they are—words from the deceiver, Satan. How can you better allow God to be in control?

Jesus…was transfigured before them…and his clothes became dazzling white…Then Peter said to Jesus…"Rabbi, it is good that we are here! …from the cloud came a voice, "This is my beloved son, listen to him." (Mark 9:2-10 NAB)

A Glimpse of Heaven
by Janie Reinart

The excitement in my daughter's voice said it all.

"Mom, I'm pregnant."

First child for her. First grandchild for me. Our joy–dazzling. We prayed for a healthy baby.

After several months, as a surprise, I mailed my daughter a box of cute maternity clothes. I never guessed that the day she received the package was the day she would start to miscarry.

Hearts broken open, our tears would not stop. Grabbing pen and paper, I wrote a lullaby for my unborn grandchild.

> Close as a whisper
> I hold you
> Gentle as a daydream
> You lean against my heart
>
> Wanting you
> Loving you
> Before you were born
> Your footprints are traced
> On my heart
> Your footprints are traced
> On my heart
>
> Sweet as a summers' day
> I breathe you in
> Soft as a lullaby
> You lean against my heart

Wanting you
Loving you
Before you were born
Your name is traced
On my heart
Your name is traced
On my heart

Tiny as a prayer
I bless you
Warm as a memory
You lean against my heart

Wanting you
Loving you
Before you were born
I know you are safe in God's arms
I know you are safe in God's arms

Hopeful for the precious gift of life, we continued to pray that my daughter would once again conceive. Several months later, I heard the words, "Mom, I'm pregnant."

As time went on, my daughter's appearance changed. Her face glowed with joy. All the while we prayed for this little one, this new miracle of life.

According to Joseph Cardinal Mindszenty, "Mothers are closer to God the Creator than any other creature: God joins forces with mothers in performing this act of creation...What on God's good earth is more glorious than this: to be a mother?"

I would answer: To be a grandmother. We welcomed our first grandson with open arms. Holding this little one close to my heart gave me a glimpse of heaven.

Reflection: Have you ever witnessed an event that gave you a glimpse of heaven? Write about a miracle that transfigured your life or the life of someone you know.

For the Jews demand signs and Greeks look for wisdom. But we proclaim Christ crucified, a stumbling block to Jews and foolishness to Gentiles. But to those who are called, Jews and Greeks alike, Christ the power of God and the wisdom of God. For the foolishness of God is wiser than human wisdom, and the weakness of God is stronger than human strength. (1 Cor. 1:22-25 NAB)

The Paradox of the Cross
by Brooke Taylor

Over the years, I have often struggled with feeling unqualified to speak on matters of faith. I hold no advanced degree. I did not attend seminary, and my understanding of theology is limited. Oftentimes, I feel God puts me in situations that merit a worthier academic mind. Yet, Paul reminds me of a different truth--a truth I see revealed in my own daughter daily. Along with her fair skin, green eyes and sandy blonde hair, my daughter Karolina is autistic. This is a lifelong, pervasive diagnosis.

I will never forget the moment when Karolina's neurologist delivered the diagnosis. Sitting in his office for what I thought would be a routine checkup, the doctor looked at me and said: "Your daughter is severely autistic. I believe she also has an intellectual disability." As my one-and-a-half-year-old daughter joyfully played in her stroller, my mind struggled to comprehend the words. He added, "We used to label this mental retardation."

Before we walked into the doctor's office, I was simply a mom with a delayed daughter. She was adopted and spent the first eleven months of her life in an orphanage. In my dreams, I had still believed she would catch up and life would be normal. Myopia has its advantages. I walked out of that office a different person.

Still struggling to breathe as I pushed Karolina in her stroller to the elevator, my stream of consciousness was a blitzkrieg of panicked thoughts. The colors suddenly drained away from the bright, vivid future I had imagined for my precious daughter.

Over the years since that diagnosis, I have likened our lives to climbing a mountain. It is slow and strenuous and often very lonely. Yet, as I climb, there are moments where I reach an opening and gaze at the valley below, the land from which we came. It is beautiful, and I know I would not have seen this scenery if God had not called us to this challenge. Life has been rich with the sweet nectar of God's grace stretching me, pulling me, and pushing me down to my knees at the foot of the cross. *I need to be there more.* Karolina possesses a natural, spontaneous faith—she does not require a supernatural sign or an understanding of the catechesis to have faith. My carefree daughter who lives without sin and teaches without words simply praises God through the story of her life.

Crucified on that Friday we call Good, Christ became disabled, paralyzed, as he hung helpless on the cross. The philosophers and prophets scoffed at this seemingly unqualified Rabbi. Yet, *in his humility,* he was never more powerful than in this moment of greatest weakness. Christ reminds us that things are not always what they may seem as he uttered, "Eloi! Eloi! Lama sabachthani?" My God, my God, why have you forsaken me? Through his ultimate surrender, he became the greatest miracle--resurrection and rebirth. So should we, follow this model as our guide to finding true wisdom as followers of the man from Galilee, the Son of God.

Reflection: Have you ever felt unqualified for a task? Through the experience, what did the Lord teach you? What new insights did the Lord reveal to you?

And as Moses lifted up the serpent in the wilderness, so must the Son of man be lifted up, that whoever believes in him may have eternal life."
For God so loved the world that he gave his only Son, that whoever believes in him should not perish but have eternal life. For God sent the Son into the world, not to condemn the world, but that the world might be saved through him. He who believes in him is not condemned; he who does not believe is condemned already, because he has not believed in the name of the only Son of God. And this is the judgment, that the light has come into the world, and men loved darkness rather than light, because their deeds were evil. For every one who does evil hates the light, and does not come to the light, lest his deeds should be exposed. But he who does what is true comes to the light, that it may be clearly seen that his deeds have been wrought in God. (John 3:14-21 RSV-CE)

Sometimes I Just Don't Get It
By Angela Miller

I have a confession to make. I have high standards. I have a vision of how everything *should* be. I may even be a not-so-closeted perfectionist. From the time I was little, I was fiercely independent and, as a teen, I remember being quoted more than once saying, "Patience is a virtue I DO NOT possess."

I am self-sufficient to a fault and I have a tendency to manage my anxieties by attempting to control the details of life. And, do you know what? To some extent, it has worked for me. I have become an expert juggler. I cram my schedule so full that it is bursting at the seams and I manage to keep checking off items on my list in rapid succession. I have a great resume, a beautiful family, and tremendous friends. I have my dream life. Yet, I find that many days, the real truth is that I look at these gifts, I look at myself, and I feel the stark emptiness of not being enough.

I love the first line of this passage. It is the closing line of Jesus' discourse with Nicodemus, a Pharisee, one of Israel's most learned men. Nicodemus had come to Jesus in the night professing that Jesus is "a teacher come from God" (John 3:4). To this, Jesus responded by explaining to Nicodemus further the realities of "heavenly things" (John 3:12). Nicodemus replied not with profound gratitude and insight, but with a question that clearly demonstrated his complete lack of understanding. The Son of God laid out before him God's plan of love and salvation and yet...Nicodemus. Just. Didn't. Get. It.

I am a Nicodemus. I apparently don't get it either. How many times have I looked upon the cross, the physical manifestation of God's love for me, and taken it for granted? How many times have I chosen the illusion of control over the freedom of surrender? How many times have I allowed my pride or the world to convince me that my worth is little more than the sum total of my achievements?

This passage boldly proclaims, "For God so loved the world that he gave his only Son" (John 3:16). For God so loved ME. I may forget this. I may not get it. But, this truth never changes.

In the cross, the Light comes into my darkness.

In the cross, I am healed.

In the cross, I am enough.

In the cross, I rejoice.

Reflection: How does God see me? Have I tied my sense of worth to my appearance, my belongings, or my achievements? How can I learn to resist the temptation of self-reliance and instead let go and trust in God and His unfailing and limitless love for me? [NOTE: The reflection questions are provided at the end of each devotion along with room for you to write. We encourage you to take the time to not just ruminate about the questions but to prayerfully invite the Holy Spirit to use your pen to uncover, reveal, inspire, surprise you with an insight, a discernment, wisdom.]

Now among those who went up to worship at the feast were some Greeks. So these came to Philip, who was from Beth-sa'ida in Galilee, and said to him, "Sir, we wish to see Jesus."

Philip went and told Andrew; Andrew went with Philip and they told Jesus.

And Jesus answered them, "The hour has come for the Son of man to be glorified. Truly, truly, I say to you, unless a grain of wheat falls into the earth and dies, it remains alone; but if it dies, it bears much fruit. He who loves his life loses it, and he who hates his life in this world will keep it for eternal life. If any one serves me, he must follow me; and where I am, there shall my servant be also; if any one serves me, the Father will honor him. (John 12:20-26 RSV)

Will to Serve
by Joan Spieth

This invitation of Jesus to follow him brings my prompt response: Of course, Lord, that is what I truly want to do! I want to follow you! However, if I'm not recognizing your voice, I may not know it is you.

A prime example of this occurred some years ago when my neighbor asked if I would care for her two young children, ages two and five. My initial answer was "No." I had a false notion that using my time to pray with people was more "valuable" than babysitting. Gratefully, God corrected my thinking!

My daughter asked if I had made a decision about my neighbor's offer. When I told her I wasn't going to do it, she simply responded, "I think you'll enjoy it, Mom."

It wasn't so much what my daughter said, but there was something in that brief conversation that rang true. It suddenly occurred to me that this was an invitation from Jesus asking me to follow Him as a caregiver to Christine and Johnny.

This job turned out never to be a burden! It became a time of joyful self-discovery, and adventure, an uncorking of a bottle of creativity as the three of us embarked on the good ship "USS Learning." It wasn't long before "letter days" became part of our routine. Loads of library books, the children's collection of Beanie Babies and their own unique ideas just kept making our days fun-filled, standing on the bow of the "USS Learning" with sights set on the next lesson.

God is the ultimate teacher--I am glad and grateful for His patience with me!

Reflection: Was there a time in your life when you made a decision only to later recognize God revealing a different direction? What was the outcome of your obedience?

Now the Passover and the Festival of Unleavened Bread were only two days away, and the chief priests and the teachers of the law were scheming to arrest Jesus secretly and kill him. "But not during the festival," they said, "or the people may riot."

While he was in Bethany, reclining at the table in the home of Simon the Leper, a woman came with an alabaster jar of very expensive perfume, made of pure nard. She broke the jar and poured the perfume on his head.

Some of those present were saying indignantly to one another, "Why this waste of perfume? It could have been sold for more than a year's wages and the money given to the poor." And they rebuked her harshly.

"Leave her alone," said Jesus. "Why are you bothering her? She has done a beautiful thing to me. The poor you will always have with you, and you can help them any time you want. But you will not always have me. She did what she could. She poured perfume on my body beforehand to prepare for my burial. Truly I tell you, wherever the gospel is preached throughout the world, what she has done will also be told, in memory of her."

Then Judas Iscariot, one of the Twelve, went to the chief priests to betray Jesus to them. (Mark 14:1-10 NASB)

Give All You Got!
by Pastor Linda C. Isaiah

When I look back over my life, I can truly say that I've been blessed!!

I have a testimony! I was raised in a little town called Waynesburg, Ohio. My father and mother were both from the Deep South and had suffered under the hands of severe racism and the Jim Crow Movement. My great grandparents were slaves. My father had a second grade education. He had to pick cotton to support his brothers and sisters. My mom finished the eighth grade then married my Dad. She was thirteen and he was 21. Momma was encouraged to do so since education wasn't in her future.

It saddens me to write this truth. But for those don't who kı believe in telling the truth! My mother had nine children. Two siblings had died as children, leaving me in a household of six t no sister.

Life was difficult!! My dad, a big strong, black man, worked at a brick yard, while my mom did house cleaning for white folk.

My dad drank in order to deal with his own inner demons and my mother found Jesus. My father beat my mother, my sibling and me often out of his frustration. I was raised in a predominantly white school and watched my very dark skinned brothers face constant discrimination. Life was hell!

In June of 1964 I began my journey of hope! My dear mother sent all of us to a Vacation Bible School at a Baptist Church, and I heard about a man named Jesus who loved me! I gave my life to Him that very day and hour. My life changed forever.

When I reflect on the story of Mary in Mark 14:1-10, giving all she had, her most expensive possession to the Master. I can relate. Can you just imagine her walking in a room full of men, full of shame and guilt, feeling unworthy to be in the Master presence, yet wanting to give all she has away because of what Jesus meant to her! Others began to speak harshly to her, but they didn't know her story. She could have held back because she was unsure of herself, but she didn't.

Because of what I've been through and more, I give all of myself and everything that I have to Jesus. He's my only HOPE!! So often people are like the disciples judging my praise to my God...I can't praise Him enough. I take the oil of my praise and worship and, as the song says,"I give myself away so He can use me!" He gave his life for this little girl, I pour my oil over and over again on his head.

Reflection: Are you giving God all He's asking you for at this particular time in your life? If not, why? If yes, what?

"I am the living bread which came down from heaven; if any one eats of this bread, he will live for ever; and the bread which I shall give for the life of the world is my flesh." The Jews then disputed among themselves, saying, "How can this man give us his flesh to eat?" So Jesus said to them, "Truly, truly, I say to you, unless you eat the flesh of the Son of man and drink his blood, you have no life in you; he who eats my flesh and drinks my blood has eternal life, and I will raise him up at the last day. For my flesh is food indeed, and my blood is drink indeed. He who eats my flesh and drinks my blood abides in me, and I in him. As the living Father sent me, and I live because of the Father, so he who eats me will live because of me. This is the bread which came down from heaven, not such as the fathers ate and died; he who eats this bread will live for ever." (John 6:51-58 RSV)

Starving for the Bread of Life
by Taylor Tripodi

When I was little, I didn't care much about what kind of food I put in my body when I was hungry. I just ate. Sometimes I would fill myself with my Mom's delicious, healthy, home-cooked Italian meals. Other times when Mom wasn't there to advise against it, I would fill myself with awful things like McDonald's chicken nuggets, candy, and chips, only to be plagued with an aching stomach afterward.

We all hunger for something. The truth is that, at the end of the day, if we don't satisfy that ache with food, we will most certainly die. Spiritual hunger is just as real. Our souls need feeding, too, yet so many of us are either starving or gorging ourselves with spiritual "fast food."

What is so beautiful about this passage in John is that Jesus refers to himself as actual LIVING bread--Food to give life to our hungry souls. He desires for us to partake of Him and even goes so far as to say that if you do not eat of this bread, His body, "you have no life within you." And he goes on to promise that if we consume this bread of life, we "will live forever." What an incredible gift--not only does Jesus promise to feed us with His own body, but He promises is that, if we do, we will live eternally with Him.

How blest we are as Christians to be able to feast on this heavenly bread through communion, daily prayer, study of the Word, and immersion into the mystery of faith.

It's time to stop attempting to fill our hungry souls with the "fast food feel-good spirituality" the world provides and stop starving ourselves spiritually by trying to be self-sufficient. It's time to eat and drink of the body of our Lord till we are overflowing with the presence of Christ each day of our lives.

Reflection: In what ways do you try to find satisfaction in the "fast food" kind of spirituality the world provides? In what ways do you try to remain self-sufficient and keep God in a box--starving yourself of the true Life He wants to give you? Do you recognize your daily need to satiate your hungry soul with Christ? How can you allow Him to feed this hunger in your day-to-day life?

Good Friday

Before the feast of Passover, Jesus knew that his hour had come to pass from this world to the Father. He loved his own in the world and he loved them to the end. The devil had already incurred Judas, son of Simon the Iscariot to hand him over. So, during supper, fully aware that the Father had put everything into his power and that he had come from God and was returning to God, he rose from supper and took off his outer garments. He took a towel and tied it around his waist. Then he poured water into a basin and began to wash the disciples' feet and dry them with the towel around his waist.

He came to Simon Peter, who said to him, "What I am doing you do not understand now, but you will understand later."

Peter said to him, "You will never wash my feet."

Jesus answered him, "Unless I wash you, you will have no inheritance with me."

Simon Peter said to him, "Master, then not only my feet, but my hands and head as well."

Jesus said to him, "Whoever has bathed has no need except to have his feet washed, for he is clean all over; so you are clean, but not all."

For he knew who would betray him; for this reason, he said, "Not all of you are clean."

So when he had washed their feet [and] put his garments back on and reclined at table again, he said to them, "Do you realize what I have done for you? You call me 'teacher' and 'master' and rightly so, for indeed I am. If I, therefore, the master and teacher, have washed your feet, you ought to wash one another's feet. I have given you a model to follow so that as I have done for you, you should also do. (John 13:1-15 NAB)

The Hands and Feet of Jesus
by Jen Gerber

As a mother, I spend most of my days serving my family. Between feeding babies, changing diapers, homeschooling, preparing meals, and folding laundry, there is always something to do. I pride myself in my ability to step up when a need arises and take care of the people around me.

In November of 2015, instead of serving, I found myself being served by others in an unimaginable and profound way. My eldest daughter had just passed away suddenly and unexpectedly and I was 29 weeks pregnant with our fifth child. Three weeks after her death, I awoke to excruciating pain in my left side. That pain turned out to be a kidney stone. I was admitted to the hospital, but my health quickly deteriorated as I developed pneumonia, low blood platelets, and went into labor at 32 weeks. I was transferred to a larger hospital where I delivered our baby boy via c-section while under general anesthesia. I didn't meet my son for the first time until the day after his birth. Two days later, I underwent surgery again to break up the large stone that still had not passed. After being released from the hospital, I spent the next several weeks traveling back and forth between home and the neonatal intensive care unit.

It was the lowest point of my entire life. I was utterly helpless and incapacitated. I could barely take care of myself let alone my family. Life was messy and broken and I didn't know how to fix it. No to do list could even contain the things that needed to be done. In that time of despair, I often wondered where Jesus was. Could He see my bleeding heart? Did He hear my cries for help?

But I simply needed to open my eyes to see Him. He was in the people bringing my family meals and gifts and caring for my children. He was there as my friends and loved ones stood vigil outside of my hospital room in prayer. His presence was manifest in the friends who drove across the country to be at my daughter's funeral and even in strangers who sent cards, e-mails, gifts, and came to the calling hours because they also knew the pain of losing a child. He heard me as I poured out my heart and my tears to my companions on this journey to the cross.

Through all of these acts of love, I recognized my Beloved, not as the all-powerful God who created the universe, but as a suffering servant, stooping down to gently wash away the dirt of a broken world. Like Peter, I found myself humbled and overwhelmed.

Family, friends, and complete strangers had been the hands and feet of Christ to me. They had followed the model that Our Lord set forth on this Holy night when He offered Himself fully and unreservedly. They had proved that when you acknowledge the suffering of another human being, when you reach out in empathy and compassion, when you become vulnerable and selflessly give of yourself to help a hurting soul, you reveal Jesus to the world.

If I, therefore, the master and teacher, have washed your feet, you ought to wash one another's feet. I have given you a model to follow so that as I have done for you, you should also do.

Reflection: How might you be the hands and feet of Christ to someone in need today? Perhaps you are the one in need. How is Christ revealing Himself to you through the service of others?

Now on the first day of the week Mary Mag'dalene came to the tomb early, while it was still dark, and saw that the stone had been taken away from the tomb. So she ran, and went to Simon Peter and the other disciple, the one whom Jesus loved, and said to them, "They have taken the Lord out of the tomb, and we do not know where they have laid him."

Peter then came out with the other disciple, and they went toward the tomb. They both ran, but the other disciple outran Peter and reached the tomb first; and stooping to look in, he saw the linen cloths lying there, but he did not go in.

Then Simon Peter came, following him, and went into the tomb; he saw the linen cloths lying, and the napkin, which had been on his head, not lying with the linen cloths but rolled up in a place by itself. Then the other disciple, who reached the tomb first, also went in, and he saw and believed; for as yet they did not know the scripture, that he must rise from the dead. (John 20:1-9 RSV)

Running to Glory
by Fr. Nathan Cromly

Today's reading is full of running! After encountering the rolled-away stone, Mary Magdalene sets off sprinting to find the disciples. Then Peter and John run as fast as their feet will carry them to Christ's tomb. Why all of this rushing about?

We know that Christians are called to "abide" in Christ, to "remain" with Him. These are terms that describe profound stability and rest. By encountering Christ's heart and personally belonging to Him— with the communion of other Christians supporting us—we enter into a profound and true rest. This element of faithfully resting in Christ is good and essential to the Christian life.

But we Christians are also called to run! In other words, loving Christ is not a static venture. Loving Christ puts a "fire in our belly:" the one who loves has to accept that thirst and desire are the new language of his heart!

Mary Magdalene's wonder at the empty tomb sends her running; so too should our wonder at earthly hints of eternity prompt us to go further. I think of how, when my MBA students encounter the beauty of Wyoming's Wind River Mountain Range on their 21-day-hiking trip starting off the school year, this beauty leads them to amazement at the author of the landscape. Then their initial encounter with the realism of beauty becomes filled with even more wonder and mystery! The things of this earth really draw them up to desire Heaven!

And yet, for all of the wonder they inspire, encounters with beauty—whether through Wyoming landscapes, Beethoven's symphonies, Michelangelo's sculptures, or even the volcanoes in Norway—leave us with a sense of incompletion, pouring into our hearts a desire greater than anyone or anything on earth can satisfy. Faced with the reality that we are made for the grandeur of intimacy in eternity, we run upward, compelled by our hunger and thirst to see Christ.

When we run to Christ, we run to the One who can repair all areas of our life that have been distorted by sin. We run to a miracle of mercy who can heal now, in this very moment of the Easter Season.

The search for lasting rest in Christ demands running, maybe not with our feet, but certainly with our intellect, will, and whole heart! Easter is a time of desire and thirst for the glory that God wishes to share with us. Let us live this season with a true thirst for the higher things, running ever nearer to glory.

Reflection: What do you desire and thirst for most in your life? What can Christ give you that will fulfill your deepest thirsts and desires?

On the evening of that day, the first day of the week, the doors being shut where the disciples were, for fear of the Jews, Jesus came and stood among them and said to them, "Peace be with you." When he had said this, he showed them his hands and his side. Then the disciples were glad when they saw the Lord. Jesus said to them again, "Peace be with you. As the Father has sent me, even so I send you." And when he had said this, he breathed on them, and said to them, "Receive the Holy Spirit. If you forgive the sins of any, they are forgiven; if you retain the sins of any, they are retained."

Now Thomas, one of the twelve, called the Twin, was not with them when Jesus came. So the other disciples told him, "We have seen the Lord." But he said to them, "Unless I see in his hands the print of the nails, and place my finger in the mark of the nails, and place my hand in his side, I will not believe."

*Eight days later, his disciples were again in the house, and Thomas was with them. The doors were shut, but Jesus came and stood among them, and said, "Peace be with you." Then he said to Thomas, "Put your finger here, and see my hands; and put out your hand, and place it in my side; do not be faithless, but believing." Thomas answered him, "My Lord and my God!" Jesus said to him, "Have you believed because you have seen me? Blessed are those who have not seen and yet believe." Now Jesus did many other signs in the presence of the disciples, which are not written in this book; but these are written that you may believe that Jesus is the Christ, the Son of God, and that believing you may have life in his name. (*John 20:19-31 RSV)

Divine Mercy, Earthly Mercy
by Marie Monsour

It was a stupid thing to do. And I will never do it again. Yet the lesson learned was far greater than, "Don't do it again." The lesson learned was Mercy. Give Mercy. Receive Mercy. Be Merciful as your heavenly Father is Merciful.

It was the fall of my junior year. I was sixteen and a "goody-two-shoes"--Good grades, good friends, involved in youth group at church. Friday night football games were the high point of the week. My friends and I would meet up and cheer on the team, then drive over to Parassons on Waterloo Rd. for food and fun.

I ate red-hots for dinner. You know, the little red cinnamon candy? No time for proper nourishment – I could wait till Parassons for a real meal. My girlfriend's boyfriend was driving and I hopped in the back seat with another friend who was also hitching a ride. "Rum and coke?" she asked. Never had I ever drank alcohol before. "Sure," I said, figuring why not? It tasted good and I had another and then finished the one my friend couldn't finish.

I won't bore you with the sordid details. You know the story – good girl gets drunk and lives to regret it. My sister dragged me home from the game and hauled me up the stairs to my bedroom. My dad's room was at the top of the steps and he was sitting at his desk. I remember the look on his face – disappointed, baffled. The rest of the night was a blur. I was very sick – let's just call it "red-hot revenge." But I often recall that night whenever I hear of a young person who has died from alcohol poisoning. It could have been me.

Monday morning at school, I was called to the principal's office. They were going to suspend me for the day – since I had no other offenses, it would be off the records but they would "make an example" out of me. That evening as I sat on my bed, my dad came into the room. He sat down next to me and chatted about the events of the weekend. I had this dreadful feeling that my whole world was about to come tumbling down. And it did. But not in the way I expected.

Dad simply said, "I think you have learned your lesson." And he left the room.

I don't think I fully understood the impact or was grateful for the mercy I had received that night until much later in my life. In fact, I think I am still feeling its effects and learning to put it into practice. The mercy God gives us is undeserved. It is often given even when the recipient is not grateful. It may even take a person a whole lifetime to recognize the mercy received. Be merciful as your heavenly Father, or even as your earthly father, is merciful.

Reflection: Have you ever experienced mercy from another person--a family member, friend, teacher, or coach? Write about a time you showed mercy to another. How does showing mercy to others mirror the mercy of God?

...Jesus was made known to them in the breaking of the bread...He stood in their midst and said to them, "Peace be with you."...he asked them. "Have you anything here to eat?" (Lk. 24:35-48 NAB)

Don't Forget
by Janie Reinart

"They're here!"

Cousins run to greet each other. Shouts and giggles mix with hugs and kisses. Peace soothes my soul as the pile of shoes at the door keeps growing. Everyone arrives safely.

Whether it's for special occasions or an ordinary day, we celebrate being together. Being together strengthens the love we share as a family. I watch everyone enjoy each other's company.

My hungry children and grandchildren live near and far. I often hear this question when we gather.

"Have you anything to eat?"

Our meals together give us a time to pray. We encourage prayer requests around the table.

My favorite prayer for the little ones is simply: "Thank you, God, for our food. Amen."

Even toddlers just learning language can imitate folding their hands and repeating, "Amen."

When they are a little older, we practice the sign of the cross.

One day, my three-year-old granddaughter and her two-year-old brother were ready to eat. The charming two-year-old was nearing the end of his stamina and needed lunch and a nap. I quickly served food and averted a melt down.

My granddaughter looked at me and said, "Grammy, don't forget the Holy Spirit!"

I apologized. "Sorry, Honey. Let's pray right now." We made the sign of the cross and said grace.

Another time, as I spread out a blanket for a picnic, my five-year-old grandson asked, "Aren't you going to pray, Grammy?"

And of course we did. We witness our faith to our families--lest we forget, our little ones will remind us.

Reflection: Remember a time your faith shines out. Take the time to reflect on how the traditions your family shares impact their spiritual formation. Which traditions do you think they will carry on?

The thief comes only to steal and kill and destroy; I have come that they may have life, and have it to the full. I am the good shepherd. The good shepherd lays down his life for the sheep. The hired hand is not the shepherd who owns the sheep. So when he sees the wolf coming, he abandons the sheep and runs away. Then the wolf attacks the flock and scatters it. The man runs away because he is a hired hand and cares nothing for the sheep. (John 10:11-18 NIV)

Ten Million Sheep on the Emerald Isle
by Robin Swoboda

I was in Ireland this past summer and as we travelled through the rich green countryside, we came upon flocks of sheep. Lots and lots of sheep grazing bucolically in the rocky, emerald fields. Ten million sheepscattered throughout the entire country! Every sheep had a large spray painted circle on its back. Blue, orange, red, blue and orange, green and purple. Some had one color. Others had two. We were told by our tour director that the color indicated who owned the sheep. One color, one owner. Two colors, two owners.

Obviously, the two colors are proof that sheep tend to wander. In fact, it wasn't uncommon to see a small group or even a single sheep running down the road in front of us.

While it was fun to watch, I had to wonder how difficult it was for the owner of the sheep to have to go out and round them all up and bring them safely home.

Jesus calls us his sheep and tells us he is the good shepherd. He did so much more than spray paint a florescent circle on our backs. He covered us in his blood on the cross.

Years ago, when I was in the midst of making a career decision that would impact my family, I heard a radio preacher say, "The sheep never makes a conscious choice of its own will to stray from the flock. It happens one nibble at a time." Not only did I see this play out in Ireland, but sadly, in my own life when I wasn't listening to his voice.

Reflection: Are you making choices that are causing you stray from his flock? What nibbles can you cut out of your life? Make a construction paper sheep and glue cotton balls to it to give it a furry feel. Now attach that sheep to your refrigerator as a reminder to keep your eye on the Shepherd in order to stay on the path—one nibble at a time.

When he [Saul] came to Jerusalem, he tried to join the disciples, but they were all afraid of him, not believing that he really was a disciple. But Barnabas took him and brought him to the apostles. He told them how Saul on his journey had seen the Lord and that the Lord had spoken to him, and how in Damascus he had preached fearlessly in the name of Jesus. So Saul stayed with them and moved about freely in Jerusalem, speaking boldly in the name of the Lord...(Acts 9:26-31 NIV)

Everyone Needs a Reliable Witness
by Judy Nagella

For as long as I can remember throughout twenty-two years of ministry, I always imagined how awesome it would be to have a "Barnabas" in my life. You know, the one chosen to come alongside to support and encourage me as I served the Lord. I always imagined this person as reliable, trustworthy, consistent and steadfast, not only in their walk with the Lord but also in their witness.

Over the years, I have learned first-hand the opposition that comes with serving the Lord. However, having a Barnabas to stand up and defend me as Barnabas did for Saul when the opposition came would have been amazing.

Yes, I longed for a trustworthy companion to guide and sustain me, like Barnabas was for Saul. Was I being prideful for having such a desire—to be loved and have someone believe in me?

One day, while sitting at the feet of Jesus, He began to speak to me. He told me He was sending me a Comforter, A Helper...could it be my Barnabas? He promised not to leave me comfortless, heartbroken, or feeling abandoned any more, and he promised that this witness would abide, dwell, and live within me forever. My heart leapt for joy...I felt so honored to receive such a wonderful gift!

I would never have imagined that the Barnabas the Lord desired to send me was not a human being, but a spiritual being...the Holy Spirit! "On that day you will realize that I am in My Father, and you are in Me, and I am in you," Jesus said (John 14:20).

Since that day, I no longer desired a "Barnabas" in my life because I received the most reliable witness anyone could ever ask for…the Holy Spirit alive within me! My life has never been the same.

When I think back over the last five years of my life, I remember a place of total darkness and despair where I did not want to go, but the Lord Jesus led me there. I found myself betrayed by a close friend. I felt hopeless, as I saw my sister and my mom struggle with health complications until the Lord took them home. Through this darkness, I had to fully rely upon Jesus. I struggled with every step. I wanted to quit. In the midst of my darkness and pain, I could hear the Lord's still small voice calling out to me. He comforted me. He mended my broken heart. He delivered me from my crushed emotions. He became my only hope, and before I knew it, He led me out of the darkness and into His Glorious Light.

By His unfailing love for me and His Holy Spirit alive within me, I have *now* become His living testimony (His reliable witness) to all the world.

Reflection: With as many details as possible, write about a time when you heard the still small voice of the Lord Jesus call out to you. How might you become a "reliable witness" for Jesus by sharing that experience from your life with someone else?

As the Father has loved me, so have I loved you; abide in my love. If you keep my commandments, you will abide in my love, just as I have kept my Father's commandments and abide in his love. These things I have spoken to you, that my joy may be in you, and that your joy may be full.

"This is my commandment, that you love one another as I have loved you. Greater love has no man than this, that a man lay down his life for his friends. You are my friends if you do what I command you. No longer do I call you servants, for the servant does not know what his master is doing; but I have called you friends, for all that I have heard from my Father I have made known to you. You did not choose me, but I chose you and appointed you that you should go and bear fruit and that your fruit should abide; so that whatever you ask the Father in my name, he may give it to you. This I command you, to love one another. (John 15:9-17 RSV)

Love, Not Control, One Another
by Katherine Szerdy

I believe there are few people in this world who have had the privilege and blessing of growing up with an idyllic childhood. And I am not one of them. My father was an alcoholic with severe anger issues while my mother was one of those extreme hoarder types that get featured on that reality TV show. So I guess you could say my siblings and I had two addicted parents. Psychologists have outlined certain personality traits based on birth order that children of addicts develop from growing up in a chaotic home, and I certainly fit the mold of the first born—over-responsible, high achieving, perfectionistic—the "savior" of the family, the child who takes attention off the family dysfunction by shining bright for all to see.

These traits served me well in coping when I was young, but as an adult, not so much. I have spent the last few decades seeking healing—deep spiritual and psychological healing--from the wounds suffered during those early years of physical and psychological abuse. Although I have experienced inner healing, I have to be honest—I have struggled to know God's love as I have struggled to know how to love others without controlling. Somehow I believe the two are connected. Jesus said they are: "This is my commandment, that you love one another as I have loved you."

Intellectually, theologically, I understand God's love. It's knowing it in my heart that had been a challenge. Yet, as I have come to more intimately know and trust my heavenly Father, as I have worked on developing a relationship with Him through attending mass (daily mass when I am able), reading the scriptures, keeping a spiritual journal, praying the rosary, I find my heart beginning to open, to let go of outgrown paradigms, and to let Him in. Only through growing in my relationship with Him have I been able to overcome the interpersonal challenges in my relationships with those I love, including with myself.

Reflection: Each day this week, that means one entry per day, spend a few minutes writing about a time that God showed you that He loves you. Don't just write a sentence. Spend time writing a brief narrative about each situation. What time of year was it? What was the weather like that day? How old were you? What were you wearing? Was anyone else with you? What was said? Did you hear God's voice, feel His presence, or did He use another person to reach out to you? Immerse yourself in the memory of God's love. Be as specific as possible. Then spend a few quiet moments allowing that memory to soak in deep.

In the first book, Theophilus, I dealt with all that Jesus did and taught until the day he was taken up, after giving instructions through the holy Spirit to the apostles whom he had chosen. He presented himself alive to them by many proofs after he had suffered, appearing to them during forty days and speaking about the kingdom of God. While meeting with them, he enjoined them not to depart from Jerusalem, but to wait for the "the promise of the Father about which you have heard me speak; for John baptized with water, but in a few days you will be baptized with the holy Spirit." When they had gathered together they asked him, "Lord, are you at this time going to restore the kingdom to Israel?" He answered them, "It is not for you to know the times or seasons that the Father has established by his own authority. But you will receive power when the holy Spirit comes upon you, and you will be my witnesses in Jerusalem, throughout Judea and Samaria, and to the ends of the earth." When he had said this, as they were looking on, he was lifted up, and a cloud took him from their sight. While they were looking intently at the sky as he was going, suddenly two men dressed in white garments stood beside them.

They said, "Men of Galilee, why are you standing there looking at the sky? This Jesus who has been taken up from you into heaven will return in the same ways as you have seen him going into heaven. (Acts 1:1-11 NAB)

Heavenly Hope
By Jen Gerber

We live on a small hobby farm nestled away in Amish country. In the stillness of a spring morning, before the chaos of homeschooling and life with five children begins, a veritable feast for the senses awaits outside my door. Chickens cluck, butterflies dance, and the smell of hay and damp earth wafts over the sun-drenched hill. Frogs emerge from the pond in a chorus of croaks, cats begin to prowl, and horses stomp impatiently as they await their morning oats. It seems all of Creation is ready to greet the day.

On these glorious mornings, despite the beauty surrounding me, I often find myself staring into the heavens desperately hoping to see something other than swirling clouds, soaring birds, and blue skies. My heart yearns for what it cannot have. I miss the girl with the contagious smile, caring heart, and love for life. My oldest daughter left this world suddenly and unexpectedly at the tender age of eleven. Her heart, so full of love for others, was unable to beat again due to a lethal and nearly undetectable heart arrhythmia. Her absence left a massive void that no amount of abundance will ever be able to fill.

As my eyes remain fixed heavenward, an involuntary tear trickles down my cheek. I wish I could grow wings and fly away from the pain of loss and separation. I am weary, and wonder how I can possibly face another day caring for my family, mending broken hearts, and leading them to Jesus under this heavy anvil of grief. It would be so much easier to simply stay here, staring into the sky.

Perhaps the disciples felt this way as they watched their Beloved fade from sight. Their grief had turned to joy as they witnessed His miraculous resurrection yet now they found themselves longing for Him again. When would He make things right? How could they accomplish the impossible task of building the Church without His presence?

In these moments of desperation, when our circumstances seem insurmountable and our hearts heavy, we need the assurance of our Hope. For the disciples, the message was relayed through two angels. For me, it takes a careful reading of God's Word, an hour spent in Adoration, or the gentle encouragement of a dear friend to remind me that He is restoring all things, even now. When I grow weary under the weight of sorrow, I can look to Him and trust that just as Jesus sent the Holy Spirit to assist the disciples in spreading the Gospel to the world, God never asks more of me than what He has empowered me to do. His Spirit lives inside of me and I too have been entrusted with the task of building His kingdom.

One day, in His perfect timing, I will witness our Lord returning as I gaze upon the heavens. All things will be made new, the work will have been accomplished, and I will see my beautiful daughter once again.

Reflection: What seemingly impossible circumstance are you facing today? What tangible steps can you take toward increasing your faith in God's promises and provision?

When the day of Pentecost had come, they were all together in one place. And suddenly a sound came from heaven like the rush of a mighty wind, and it filled all the house where they were sitting. And there appeared to them tongues as of fire, distributed and resting on each one of them. And they were all filled with the Holy Spirit and began to speak in other tongues, as the Spirit gave them utterance.

Now there were dwelling in Jerusalem Jews, devout men from every nation under heaven. And at this sound the multitude came together, and they were bewildered, because each one heard them speaking in his own language. And they were amazed and wondered, saying, "Are not all these who are speaking Galileans? And how is it that we hear, each of us in his own native language? Par'thians and Medes and E'lamites and residents of Mesopota'mia, Judea and Cappado'cia, Pontus and Asia, Phryg'ia and Pamphyl'ia, Egypt and the parts of Libya belonging to Cyre'ne, and visitors from Rome, both Jews and proselytes, Cretans and Arabians, we hear them telling in our own tongues the mighty works of God." (Acts 2:1-11 RSV)

Desperate for More!
by Pastor Linda C. Isaiah

Taking care of my mother wasn't always easy. It came with challenges. Mamma was starting to be forgetful and confused. At the time, I was working at a daycare and having financial struggles. With my mother living in Canton and me in Akron, it made it hard for me to care for her. Most days I would work all day and go to check on her after work. Did I mention that my marriage was in trouble? My brothers and I had to make the decision to move her closer to me since I would be the one taking care of her. So we moved her and eventually Mama worsened and had to be placed in a care facility.

My heart was broken. I was exhausted. I was overwhelmed. I was tired. I knew she was progressing in her diagnosis of Alzheimer's, but this seemed so sudden. Alzheimer's was robbing me of my precious, kind, caring, compassionate, considerate, God-fearing mother.

As I was driving in my blue 5-speed, 2-door Mercury Topaz, I began to cry uncontrollably. I pulled over to the nearest rest stop and cried, cried and cried some more. I asked God, "It seems like I just don't have enough of you to get through this trial. I don't feel you. Where are you?"

As I sat sobbing, I could feel the Lord hovering over me like a father would his child. He whispered in my ear, "Leave it all here. Just call on my name."

I began to call on Jesus, and words that I have never heard before, had never spoke before, began to come out of my mouth! I was speaking in tongues. There was a presence in that car as if He and I were the only two people in the world. The more I cried, the more the words that I've never been taught flowed like a river of life. I believe God was giving me more! I believe there is more!! I wanted more!!!

When your heart gets on one accord with the Lord and you yearn for more, it comes. Let me say that has been my experience. I felt a filling, an anointing like never before. It was extraordinary! Now I know there are many theological debates about these issues. I'm just sharing what has been real to me. Act 2: 1-11 speaks about The Day of Pentecost!

I don't know about you, but I want all God has for me! Tongues, Holy Water and all!

Reflection: Have you ever had a spiritual experience that you can't explain? If so, what? Try to recall the experience in living color and draw or paint a picture of it. If you cannot recall an experience of your own, try to recall a spiritual experience that happened to someone else. Record it here—in words or colors!

For all who are led by the Spirit of God are sons of God. For you did not receive the spirit of slavery to fall back into fear, but you have received the spirit of sonship. When we cry, "Abba! Father!" it is the Spirit himself bearing witness with our spirit that we are children of God, and if children, then heirs, heirs of God and fellow heirs with Christ, provided we suffer with him in order that we may also be glorified with him. (Romans 8:14-17 RSV)

Loved Times Three
by Jeff Cavins

As I think about the basic needs of life and the desired atmosphere of a family, I would have to say that the priority is not to be rich, well clothed, possessing a large home, but the priority is to create an atmosphere of love and acceptance.

Trinity Sunday is a reminder that we have been called to participate in the love of God. The love of the Trinity has often been described as the Father eternally loving His son, Jesus. Jesus eternally loves the Father and the love between them is the Holy Spirit. We were created to share in the life of the Trinity, which is an invitation to be saturated in godly love. Perfect love drives out fear (1 John 4:18) so this week, as you are walking in God's love, resist fear and accept your security in the Trinity.

St. Paul reminds us that our relationship with God is a relationship with three persons, the Father, Son and Holy Spirit. We are led by the Spirit of God and have received the spirit of adoption. Our cry to God is a cry from his adopted children to a Father who deeply loves us and chose to adopt us. We have been adopted into the life of the Trinity because of love and for love. The first paragraph of the Catholic Catechism elaborates on the truths found in this week's readings. "God, infinitely perfect and blessed in himself, in a plan of sheer goodness freely created man to make him share in his own blessed life." God "invites men to become, in the Holy Spirit, his adopted children and thus heirs of his blessed life."

Knowing that God has "a plan of sheer goodness" for his children, we can eagerly approach Him as a loved child rather than as a slave. Though the Trinity can be a difficult concept to get our minds around, we can accept that each person of the Trinity wants us to be part of the family of God as His child. To sum up this week's readings...we are so loved.

Reflection: If you knew that God was inviting you into a family of infinite love, how would that change your day? Be specific. Envision it. Write about it.

Brothers and sisters:

   When Christ came as high priest of the good things that have come to be, passing through the greater and more perfect tabernacle not made by hands, that is, not belonging to this creation, he entered once for all into the sanctuary, not with the blood of goats and calves but with his own blood, thus obtaining eternal redemption.

   For if the blood of goats and bulls and the sprinkling of a heifer's ashes can sanctify those who are defiled so that their flesh is cleansed, how much more will the blood of Christ, who through the eternal Spirit offered himself unblemished to God, cleanse our consciences from dead works to worship the living God.

   For this reason he is mediator of a new covenant: since a death has taken place for deliverance from transgressions under the first covenant, those who are called may receive the promised eternal inheritance.
(Hebrews 9:11-15 NABRE)

This is My Body, This is My Blood
by Marie Monsour

   I heard a priest recently talking about the mystery of suffering and the idea of offering our sufferings to God. He took issue with the idea of "offering it up" preferring rather the idea of *uniting* our sufferings *with* Christ as scripture seems to suggest (Col. 1:24, Eph 3:10).

   Understanding that our sufferings have worth, have value when united to the sufferings of Christ changes our whole mindset. The feast of the Body and Blood of Christ seems to me a good time to take stock of how I can unite my bodily sufferings (even though they may be quite small!) with the body of Christ. Fulton Sheen said that at the moment in Mass where the priest repeats the words of Christ, we ought to be saying the same: "This is *my* body, which is given up for you...this is *my* blood..." laying our very selves on the paten as we go forward to receive His precious Body and Blood.

My college-aged son took a job at a rolling door factory one summer. He learned quite a bit about suffering that summer. It was grueling work, and his knuckles would often be bloody by the end of the work day. It didn't take him long before he wrote these lines. Would that our every day hardships and difficulties would always remind us of the One who endured the greatest suffering that we might be united with Him in heaven one day.

Dunnage
by James Monsour

Keep on rolling the cart,
Down the aisles of doors,
Where the stacks are assorted
On rollers and floors.

As for some come the forklifts,
The others are bourne
By the joint-strained and
Bone-sored appendages worn.

Bring the doors, and the track,
Bring the tortions, on rack,
And the beams and the rails,
And the hardware like nails!

And the voice of the metal
That clangs like a wrack,
With its clamoring, clamoring,
"Dunnage boards back!"

Fill the truck, fill the spaces
With foam and with bags,
And refill them with air
So they're tight in the crags.

And after the bundles,
And after the track,
The dunnage boards wait
For their trip to the rack.

The nine-footers, eight-footers,
Junk-yard ensembles
Of plywood for bolstering
Rolling door bundles.

The twelve-foot, sixteen-foot,
All servant to us,
Yet beneath the oak dunnage
Lies dunnage-skin bust.

I know of a man who was
Dunnage for me;
While he bore me to safety,
Was racked to a tree.

His bones and his tendons
Became like the wood,
The splinters he gathered
Conformed to his good.

Became he the dunnage board
On which he hung,
And I the poor rolling door
Whose weight him rung.

If I could be like the dunnage board tree,
and fixed to supporting
The weight of the rest,
Perhaps I'd transfigure my splinters to ash,
and easier bear
The weight of my test.

Reflection: Do I see my every day tasks, especially the most bitter and difficult ones, as *potential*? Do I see them in light of the sufferings Christ bore on the Cross? How does that change my perspective toward hardship and sufferings I endure from day to day?

Out of the depths I cry to thee, O Lord!
Lord, hear my voice!
Let thy ears be attentive
to the voice of my supplications!

If thou, O Lord, shouldst mark iniquities,
Lord, who could stand?
But there is forgiveness with thee,
that thou mayest be feared.

I wait for the Lord, my soul waits,
and in his word I hope;
my soul waits for the Lord
more than watchmen for the morning,
more than watchmen for the morning.

O Israel, hope in the Lord!
For with the Lord there is steadfast love,
and with him is plenteous redemption.
And he will redeem Israel
from all his iniquities.   (Psalm 130: 1-8 RSV-CE)

The Power of His Whisper
by Melody Lyons

I sat in the back of the church and felt sobs rising from deep within. The urge was so abrupt and overpowering that I almost ran out the back door to save myself the humiliation. But I stayed and tried to breathe while I pressed an old ratty tissue hard into my eyes. It had a stale piece of gum stuck in the middle of it--who knows how old and to which kid it belonged--but it was all I could find in my pockets. I didn't know I would need a tissue today.

That was the day God revealed Himself to me after months of hiding. I don't really know if He'd been hiding. Perhaps I just had my eyes so focused on the ground, taking it one step at a time, struggling to hold myself up, that I couldn't see Him. Wouldn't see Him. It had been many months of knowing and believing He must be there even though I could not feel His presence. Those dry times burn.

What do you mean I might have to die to find relief? That is too hard. That is for saints... and I am not a saint.

Through the years, I have hoped for consolation during hard times but I know it's impossible to summon the action of God as if He's a genie in a bottle. We cannot order consolation as if they were a hamburger. He is not a puppet but a Lover. Not a formula but a burning fire. I pray continually for respite from sorrow or sickness... but it must come in His way and His time.... Unexpectedly. Tenderly. Powerfully. Perfectly.

So I sat in my pew, unsuspecting and silent; and without a word He revealed His Presence to my soul. And I crumpled and wept as He swept in like a mighty rain shower, quenching my parched spirit and caught me unprepared by *the power of His whisper*. How many opportunities to love Him that I have missed! How often I have felt contempt toward myself, ashamed of my helplessness... and perhaps toward Him.

And still He came.

My cross had seemed unusually heavy in recent months--only He can relieve the burden, soothe and heal my soul. I don't handle waiting well. *True relief is not an absence of suffering...but the very Presence of Jesus Christ. He is enough.*

Reflection: Are you currently enduring a heavy suffering without any sign of relief? Write a letter to God asking for the courage to wait in patient hope.

Brothers and sisters:
We are always courageous, although we know that while we are at home in the body we are away from the Lord, for we walk by faith, not by sight. Yet we are courageous, and we would rather leave the body and go home to the Lord. Therefore, we aspire to please him, whether we are at home or away. For we must all appear before the judgment seat of Christ, so that each may receive recompense, according to what he did in the body, whether good or evil. (2 Corinthians 5:6-10 NAB-RE)

Our Bodies, Our Homes
by Tanya Weitzel

We are each given homes in which to live on this Earth. These homes are our bodies, special temples that God commanded us to care for and love. I have abused and mistreated mine over the years through self-hatred and negative thoughts. I have never fully loved the body I was given. I am just now beginning to learn to accept it as my home. It is a very long journey.

My actions of not taking care of my body kept me from becoming close to God. I was rejecting God by not accepting myself. Preoccupied with my own body, I would constantly compare my appearance with others. I didn't see whole people, only the bodies they occupied. As I am better at accepting myself, I find it easier to see people for who they are, not just their outer frames. Our temples were chosen for us by God. They are his gifts to us. By rejecting our gifts, we reject God.

Reflection: What sinful tendencies hold you back from accepting God's gifts, God's love for you? How can you better accept and use what God has already given you?

In the time of Herod king of Judea there was a priest named Zechariah, who belonged to the priestly division of Abijah; his wife Elizabeth was also a descendant of Aaron. Both of them were righteous in the sight of God, observing all the Lord's commands and decrees blamelessly. But they were childless because Elizabeth was not able to conceive, and they were both very old.

Once when Zechariah's division was on duty and he was serving as priest before God, he was chosen by lot, according to the custom of the priesthood, to go into the temple of the Lord and burn incense. And when the time for the burning of incense came, all the assembled worshipers were praying outside.

Then an angel of the Lord appeared to him, standing at the right side of the altar of incense. When Zechariah saw him, he was startled and was gripped with fear. But the angel said to him: "Do not be afraid, Zechariah; your prayer has been heard. Your wife Elizabeth will bear you a son, and you are to call him John. He will be a joy and delight to you, and many will rejoice because of his birth, for he will be great in the sight of the Lord. He is never to take wine or other fermented drink, and he will be filled with the Holy Spirit even before he is born. He will bring back many of the people of Israel to the Lord their God. And he will go on before the Lord, in the spirit and power of Elijah, to turn the hearts of the parents to their children and the disobedient to the wisdom of the righteous—to make ready a people prepared for the Lord." (Luke 1:5-17)

Just Call Me "Jo Jo"
by Joy Trachsel

I will never forget the morning when we received the call from my daughter. The sweet nervous voice on the other end of the phone said, "She is on her way."

Within the hour, I was packed and in the car ready to make the five-hour drive to Indiana. After arriving at the hospital, we settled in for the wait for our first grandchild. The other grandmother and I couldn't wait any longer, so we snuck back to the delivery room in hopes of getting the news that our granddaughter had arrived. After a caregiver gently reminded us where we were not supposed to be, we returned and continued our wait.

Within a few hours, we received the news and ran back to see this precious baby girl. Words cannot express the love I immediately felt for this child. I had only known her for a few minutes, but felt like I had loved her forever. I yearned for the moment she would look at me and call me "Jo Jo" for the first time.

We had months to prepare for the arrival of this cutie and to dream big dreams for her. When Zechariah received the word of his future son, he was given detailed prophecies regarding what his son would accomplish and how he would minister. How comforting it must have been to know that a child would be born and to know the impact he would make. We each have great dreams for our children but our primary prayer should be that they impact others and further God's kingdom. Take a moment today and think of a child that is under your influence. Pray that the Lord uses them in a big way to minister in His name.

Reflection: Write about a time when you anticipated an upcoming event. How did God reveal Himself to you and affirm His presence in your life?

You have changed my sadness into a joyful dance;
You have taken away my sorrow
And surrounded me with joy.
So I will not be silent;
I will sing praise to you.
Lord, you are my God;
I will give you thanks forever. (Psalms 30:11-12 GNT-CE)

Living Joyfully
By Jenni Ellis

Salutations and closures in email have always been important to me. A salutation in an email is a way to say hello before jumping into the topic at hand. A closure is a way to say goodbye.

For some crazy reason the rules for email seem to be different than face-to-face interaction. If we say hello and goodbye when we are speaking with someone in-person, why wouldn't we do the same in an email?

I have read hundreds of thousands of emails and almost as many different salutations and closures have been used. While I appreciate a salutation, I find the closures to be more reflective of the person sending the email. As the last note of a song stays with you, the closure of an email can do the same thing.

It took me many years to determine what my personal closure for email was going to be. "Cheers" didn't work because it sounded like an invitation to have a drink with me. "All the best" didn't work because I felt that it meant that I wouldn't be in contact with that person again for a very long time. "Yours truly" didn't fit, especially in a work environment and, in the same way, "Love" wasn't appropriate either. I felt "In Christ," "In His Name" and other similar closures came off as a bit too preachy.

How could I close my emails in a way that reflected who I am? More importantly, how could I close my emails as a way to express who God is calling me to be?

You have changed my sadness into a joyful dance; you have taken away my sorrow and surrounded me with joy. So I will not be silent; I will sing praise to you. Lord, you are my God; I will give you thanks forever (Psalm 30:11-12).

Joy – a small, three-letter word that speaks volumes. God wants me to be filled with joy no matter what. And it is He who brings me joy. No matter what external circumstances are occurring in my life, it is the internal joy that permeates my relationship with God that I want to radiate through all I do, even my emails.

Reflection: What word or phrase sums up who God is calling you to be? In what way can you incorporate this word or phrase into your day-to-day life? To help you incorporate this word or phrase, create a collage about it incorporating magazine clippings, washi tape, photographs, sketches.

My grace is sufficient for you, for power is made perfect in weakness.
(2 Corinthians 12: 7-10 RSV)

From Clown to Mom!
by Betty Schnitzler

"What do you want to be when you grow up?" We have all been asked this question sometime during childhood, and we have asked children in our lives this same question.

For me, the answer changed, from when I was a young child when I wanted to be a clown (because who does not want their lives to be all fun and games) to when I started school and played school with my friends. Then I wanted to become a teacher because I loved arts and crafts!

As a teen with baby twin sisters, I started babysitting and spending a lot of time with neighbor families who had small children and babies. Then all I wanted to be was a wife and to carry a baby in my womb and be a mom!

I was blessed to find a potential husband, a young man who was also from a large family and who also wanted to have children.

This dream of having a large family changed in one afternoon at a routine doctor's appointment when I was told that I had endometriosis and that if we wanted to attempt to have children, we should start a family right NOW.

Sometimes the choices we make in life are good for us and sometimes they are not in our best interest. The Lord, in His perfect timing, stepped in and let me know that no matter how set I was on the plans in my head and my heart, it was His plan and His timing that was important. Even though I was never able to carry a child in my womb, God did indeed allow me to be a mom, through adoption, three times over! Our children were not carried in my body, but they have certainly always been carried in my heart! He has since blessed us richly, with a precious granddaughter who is the light of our lives.

Attempting to be strong in my faith during the difficult years of our early marriage was a challenge! We struggled in many areas because of infertility issues. We knew that God was with us and blessing us with His grace, but in our weakness we needed His grace to make us strong!

Reflection: What seemingly insurmountable issues can you turn over to the Lord right now? Show him your weakness and he will show you His strength. Jot them down on paper and shred them in your paper shredder or burn in your fireplace (supervised, of course!). WARNING: Do not recycle "insurmountable issues"!

In Him we have redemption through his blood, the forgiveness of sins, in accordance with the riches of God's grace that he lavished on us.
(Ephesians 1:7-8 NIV)

Christmas in July
by Trish Berg

Christmas is my favorite time of year. I love the little white lights that adorn our banister, the garland we hang over the doorway, our Christmas trees and the smell of pine and peppermint that permeate the whole house. When our children were little, our Christmas celebrations began as soon as Thanksgiving ended. I would gather up all their favorite children's books, especially the ones about Christmas or winter, individually wrap them in Christmas wrapping paper, and pile them in a basket next to the Christmas tree. Each night before bed, they were allowed to open one book and that would be their bedtime story. Occasionally, I would add a brand-new book, but most of the books were the old favorites. Unwrapping a book each night brought the kids so much joy because it was a "gift" specially wrapped for them.

On Christmas Eve day, we would bake cookies and get the house ready for the big day. After supper, we would get all dressed up in our holiday outfits and head to church for Christmas Eve service. Church was always special as we sang traditional Christmas hymns and were reminded of the gift God "specially wrapped" for us in swaddling cloth, laid in a manger. The last song was always *Silent Night* as the lights were dimmed and the candles were lit one by one, creating a beautiful vision of glowing faces, joy-filled eyes and beautiful smiles.

We would drive home as the kids chattered and giggled in the back seat. They would talk about where Santa might be flying with his sleigh full of toys. Their excitement was palpable and even contagious. Once we got home, they each opened one gift, new Christmas pajamas. They would race upstairs to put them on and then join us at the kitchen table for a Christmas cookie, a cup of hot cocoa (with marshmallows, of course), and a reading of *T'was the Night Before Christmas.* Then it was off to bed with a kiss, a prayer and a Christmas-sized dream.

Christmas morning always dawned early as the kids were so eager they could hardly wait to get us up. They would run into our bedroom and jump on our bed at dawn, then toddle downstairs to find the Christmas tree surrounded by wrapped presents and the banister adorned with overflowing stockings. Their joy and wonderment reflected their excitement over being lavished with gifts Christmas morning.

If only we could capture that feeling of being lavished every day. Somewhere along our growing up path, we forget what it feels like to be lavished with gifts. We grow up and we grow stagnant in our joy. But God wants us to feel lavished. He lavishes us with the riches of His grace and the forgiveness found only in Jesus. That is what grace is. What our redemption in Jesus is. In fact, our redemption should feel like Christmas morning.

So maybe it's time to celebrate Christmas in July. Maybe we need to be reminded of God's grace, which He lavishes on us. So, bake some Christmas cookies, make some hot cocoa (with marshmallows, of course), and put on your comfy pajamas. Read through the story of Jesus' birth (Luke 2:1-20) and ask God to remind you of your worth to Him. Allow the gift of Jesus to bring you the joy of Christmas every day of the year. Allow yourself to feel lavished by His grace, like a cool winter breeze on a hot July day. Merry Christmas!

Reflection: What Christmas traditions does your family have that exemplify the joy you feel at Christmastime? Write about three ways you can capture the child-like joy of Christmas morning throughout the year.

The Lord is my shepherd;
I have all that I need.
He lets me rest in green meadows;
he leads me beside peaceful streams.
He renews my strength.
He guides me along right paths,
bringing honor to his name.
Even when I walk through the darkest valley,
I will not be afraid, for you are close beside me.
Your rod and your staff protect and comfort me.
You prepare a feast for me in the presence of my enemies.
You honor me by anointing my head with oil.
My cup overflows with blessings.
Surely your goodness and unfailing love will pursue me all the days of
my life, and I will live in the house of the Lord forever." (Psalms 23:1-6
NLT)

Home Sweet Home?
Ruth Clifford

As I was thinking of this scripture, I couldn't help but think about a time when I found myself in a desperate situation needing urgent help. It was Good Friday and I was eight months pregnant with my second child. I awoke and checked my email first thing, as is my typical routine, and was shocked to discover an email from our landlord saying that he was going to sell his house and we needed to be out by June 1st—my due date! We had just painted the nursery the weekend before and we were excited to get things in order weeks before the birth. I thought I was getting ready to "nest!" I immediately broke into tears and ran into the bedroom to share the news with my husband.

Our first instinct was to try to fix the problem ourselves. I called our friend, Judy, who is a realtor to ask her for her help. We called the landlord to ask him for more time. We called our parents. It seemed that we talked to everyone except the One who knew best what to do. Instead of putting it all in God's hands, we tried to take control of the situation and let it completely consume us.

With our busy schedules and a baby on the way, before we knew it, we were down to the wire. With two days left to find a house, I called our realtor Judy again, crying that we needed to make a miracle happen. She told me not to worry--that God would take care of us. And as usual, He did!

I have learned that God specializes in miracles. When we are most desperate, that is when He is nearest. Or shall I say, that is when we need Him most. We recognize in those desperate moments that God is truly our shepherd, watching over us all the time, even in our valley moments-when we feel our lowest and alone--He is STILL there, working on a miracle.

How does the story end? We found a house on the second day. We were able to close on the house and move in, and our baby boy, Gabriel, was born a week later. God had a plan the entire time!

Reflection: (1) Reflect on a time when God was your Shepherd, watching over you and protecting you and write about it here. (2) The version of the 23rd Psalm offered here is a modern paraphrase, the New Living Translation, put in 21st century language. Sometimes reading a different version of the scriptures casts a spotlight on the message, providing a fresh look at a passage we may have read many times and revealing something we may not have noticed before. What part of this version of Psalm 23 stands out to you today?

After this, Jesus went across the Sea of Galilee [of Tiberias]. A large crowd followed him, because they saw the signs he was performing on the sick. Jesus went up on the mountain, and there he sat down with his disciples. The Jewish feast of Passover was near. When Jesus raised his eyes and saw that a large crowd was coming to him, he said to Philip, "Where can we buy enough food for them to eat?" He said this to test him, because he himself knew what he was going to do. Philip answered him, "Two hundred days' wages worth of food would not be enough for each of them to have a little [bit]." One of his disciples, Andrew, the brother of Simon Peter, said to him, "There is a boy here who has five barley loaves and two fish; but what good are these for so many?" Jesus said, "Have the people recline." Now there was a great deal of grass in that place. So the men reclined, about five thousand in number. Then Jesus took the loaves, gave thanks, and distributed them to those who were reclining, and also as much of the fish as they wanted. When they had had their fill, he said to his disciples, "Gather the fragments left over, so that nothing will be wasted." So they collected them, and filled twelve wicker baskets* with fragments from the five barley loaves that had been more than they could eat. When the people saw the sign he had done, they said, "This is truly the Prophet, the one who is to come into the world." Since Jesus knew that they were going to come and carry him off to make him king, he withdrew again to the mountain alone. (John 6: 1-15)

Jesus Wants to Feed Us!
Give Him Your Yes
by Emily Jaminet

Jesus feeding the 5,000 is one of my favorite miracles. What a glorious thing that Jesus was able to meet the physical needs of the people gathered! He started the miracle with the fundamental question that I too have pondered in my own life as a mother with a large family, "Where can we buy enough food for them to eat?" Now the Gospel even tells us that he was testing the disciples. Did Jesus want to see their reaction or allow the disciples to experience the need to depend on Christ for not only matters of faith but for their own physical needs as well?

Nothing has stretched my faith more than providing for the physical and spiritual needs of seven children ranging in age from one to eighteen. Each child's needs are complex--whether physical, spiritual, emotional or even mental health needs! We as parents have a tremendous responsibility to help our children. But just think! Christ wants to care for us caregivers too, like we do for our children and loved ones!

Christ wants us to turn to him and seek his help and guidance in all matters, even the basic needs of our daily necessities. Remember, providing for our physical needs is not a matter of whether we live on a budget or not, but rather if we are willing to say thank you for our daily blessings and seek Christ's help in all things. When Christ asked God the Father to bless the small loaves of bread from a young child, he was able to produce a mighty miracle. The food did not multiply until after he said thank you! Our thanks to God and others is a powerful way to gain God's attention and allow him to impact our lives!

In life, Jesus takes care of us when we are willing to give him our yes and hand over the complexity of our lives and allow him to help us.

Reflection: What areas of my life do I need to ask Jesus for his help? Do I believe that he can meet my physical needs as much as my spiritual needs?

Jesus said to them, "I am the bread of life; whoever comes to me will never hunger, and whoever believes in me will never thirst." (John 6:35 NAB)

Filled by the Eucharist
by Michele Faehnle

I grew up in a large Catholic family, the oldest of eight children. My parents were very devout and strongly believed in the importance of the Eucharist, so it seemed like every night we were doing something religious. We attended daily mass, Holy Hour once a week, and Charismatic healing masses on a regular basis. Although I was exposed to "the source and summit of the Christian life" on a daily basis, I didn't get it. As a young child I was curious about God and my faith, but by the time I was a teenager, I was just bored. Instead of using that time to pray and commune with God, all I could think about was how I couldn't wait to get home to call my friends or current boyfriend. I went along with my parents' wishes to placate them so they would let me do what I wanted on the weekends. Although I knew my faith was the truth, I hadn't fallen in love with Jesus yet.

At the ripe old age of seventeen, I went to college. Living seven hours away from my family and friends, I quickly found myself in a place of deep loneliness. Although I was surrounded by fellow students, I missed the close relationships that had filled my life up to that point. I busied myself with schoolwork and a heavy dose of the party life to fill the void, but only found myself more and more unsatisfied. One night, sitting alone in my dorm room, I felt completely empty. Not knowing what to do or where to turn, I wandered outside the dorm and began walking the campus.

A short walk later, I found myself in front of the Eucharistic Adoration chapel and I felt drawn to enter. I entered the silent room filled with students in prayer, sank down in a pew facing the gleaming gold monstrance and began to pour out my heart to Jesus. In that moment I was filled with a warm consolation; a pervading peace that I knew was the hand of God. It was in that moment I experienced Christ in the Eucharist like I never had before and my life was changed forever.

Now I run to the Eucharist and can't wait to attend mass and spend quiet moments sharing my life with Jesus in adoration. It is there that I find my strength and my meaning. Now, I no longer hunger and thirst, for I know where I can be filled to overflowing.

Reflection: Do you hunger and thirst for Jesus? Tell him here and now in the form of a written prayer. How has the Eucharist changed you?

I will bless the LORD at all times;
  his praise shall be always in my mouth.
My soul will glory in the LORD;
  let the poor hear and be glad.
Magnify the LORD with me;
  and let us exalt his name together.
I sought the LORD, and he answered me,
  delivered me from all my fears.
Look to him and be radiant,
  and your faces may not blush for shame.
This poor one cried out and the LORD heard,
  and from all his distress he saved him.
The angel of the LORD encamps
  around those who fear him, and he saves them.
Taste and see that the LORD is good;
  blessed is the stalwart one who takes refuge in him.
  (Psalm 34:2-9 NAB)

Who Am I?
by Joan Spieth

Most of us love to plan for or be a part of a celebration. I have a good friend who seems so full of joy and enthusiasm that I believe "Celebrate" must be her middle name! The current of her positive energy and spirit of hospitality connects everyone with a sense of belonging. She always seems to have something to celebrate. These spiritual gifts are an important part of who God created my friend to be and for which she will always be remembered.

Celebrations are a cherished part of our lives. We come together to celebrate the union of husband and wife or the entrance of a precious baby into the world. We celebrate in community as we "Welcome to the Neighborhood, Friend" in the spirit of Mr. Rogers or say goodbye to old friends around the campfire, "Happy Trails until We Meet Again," as Roy Rogers and Dale Evans sang in harmony.

The Mass of Resurrection is the final celebration of a person's life. There have been times I've been honored with an invitation to write and give a eulogy. Within that process, the question always stares me in the face: "What would I want to have said about me?"

A few hours of deep pondering produced the ideal answer: "She was grateful and glad." This insight has helped me to embrace my identity in Christ as well as to give direction to my life.

Reflection: What Christ-like qualities would you most want to be remembered for? Would you prayerfully consider your own life's caption? How specifically might you live to earn that description? A suggested creative activity: Make a Word Cloud of the qualities you identified. Go to www.wordle.net and follow the user-friendly directions for creating your word cloud. You can print it out and frame it or laminate it as a reminder of those qualities.

Look carefully then how you walk, not as unwise men but as wise, making the most of the time, because the days are evil. Therefore do not be foolish, but understand what the will of the Lord is. And do not get drunk with wine, for that is debauchery; but be filled with the Spirit, addressing one another in psalms and hymns and spiritual songs, singing and making melody to the Lord with all your heart, always and for everything giving thanks in the name of our Lord Jesus Christ to God the Father. (Ephesians 5:15-20)

Preventative or Curative?
by Leah Cheng

"Be careful then how you live, not as unwise but as wise." St. Paul is speaking of being wise in the ways of God and His ways do not coincide with the ways of the world. The ways of God and those of the world are in every way opposed to one another. According to Matthew, "No one can serve two masters. Either you will hate the one and love the other, or you will be devoted to the one and despise the other. You cannot serve both God and mammon" (Matt 6:24). In his book, *The Gift of Faith*, Father Tadeusz Dajczer states, "There are *two* masters--God and mammon. There is no third....The relationship of one master to the other is a relationship of *radical contradiction*" (emphasis mine). There are no compromises. You choose God or you choose something that is not God. "To choose Christ as the supreme value" is a daily choice which requires surrender, love and trust (Dajczer).

Radical surrender.

Radical love.

Radical trust.

Our beloved and venerable saints did not become so through com-promise. Going back as far as Moses, God asks for love without com-promise in Deut 6:5, "You shall love the Lord your God with *all* your heart, with *all* your soul and with *all* your strength." He means it. Take a look at Abraham and see how *comprehensive* is the love and trust God desires, even demands, from those He calls. First, Abraham is asked to leave nearly everything he knows, everything he is familiar with in order to begin a new life in another land. If that wasn't challenging enough, God later asks him to sacrifice his only son and heir! No compromise here.

Many things divide our hearts, our souls and our strength here in this earthly life. In this letter to the Ephesians, St Paul exhorts his hearers not to "get drunk on wine which leads to debauchery." The words "drunk", "wine" and "debauchery" can be replaced with words such as possessed by, obsessed with, overly concerned with....fashion, beauty, food, fitness, wealth management, shopping, knowledge, television, sports, social networking--name your indulgences and addictions, perhaps your job, even things you simply enjoy--which leads to, well, sin, to be blunt, whether by commission or omission. These things in and of themselves are not necessarily evil, but when they begin to fill that hole in our lives reserved for God, we violate the First Commandment. In his second letter to the Corinthians, St Paul is even more emphatic: Let us purify ourselves from *everything* which contaminates body and soul, perfecting holiness *out of reverence for God*" (2 Cor 7:1).

Christ Himself speaks of detachment in striking language. "Our adherence to Christ is not possible without detaching ourselves from whatever can enslave us," asserts Fr. Dajczer. "Woe to the world because of the things that cause people to stumble...If your hand or your foot causes you to stumble, cut it off and throw it away...And if your eye causes you to stumble, gouge it out and throw it away!" No compromise. Again, the Lord is trying to impress upon us the totality of surrender, the love and trust He desires--and knows that we *need* in order to exercise power over temptation and sin as well as to grow in our knowledge, love and service of God. This is akin to stressing preventative care over curative treatment. Remove temptations to sin and those obstacles and distractions that stunt our spiritual growth from our daily routine.

Reflection: Where in your life are you compromising? Where are you choosing to serve mammon instead of God? If you struggle to find time to pray, evaluate where your time is spent. If you struggle to tithe or increase your tithe, evaluate where you money goes. Are you more concerned about the approval of people or God? Who do you consult with first? Friends, colleagues, or God?

God won't put up with rebels; he'll cull them from the pack. Is anyone crying for help? God is listening, ready to rescue you. (Psalms 34:16-17 MSG)

When God Speaks
by Lori Triplett

Several years ago, I had come very close to leading a completely different life than I do today. I was over ten years deep into what had become an emotionally abusive and toxic relationship. I had become engaged and had completely lost myself in the relationship somewhere along the way. My self-worth was at an all-time low, and although I was miserable, I was too embarrassed and terrified to start over. Where would I even begin? I had left my pursuit of a music career behind in Nashville to move to Cleveland, Ohio, for him and had completely fallen into his life at the expense of my own calling, my dreams.

He was on staff at the church I was attending and actively involved in, so when I broke things off, I had intended to stop attending the church eventually. However, in my brokenness, I needed my church family and continued attending. Then one day I was told by my pastor that I could no longer sing there and that I should leave the church. "There are lots of churches in Cleveland," my pastor said to me in one of my most vulnerable times. To say I was deeply hurt would be an incredible understatement.

During this transition, I moved in with close friends. One day I had the house to myself and experienced one of the most intimate moments with the Lord. On my hands and knees, I sobbed and prayed. In my desperation and fear of the unknown, I had been trying to save the relationship into which I had invested so much of myself. I was willing to fight for it, but he was not. Over and over, I cried out, "Why won't he fight for me? Why am I not worth it?" I was angry at him, my church, and the friends who had abandoned me. I wanted to lash out at everyone and tell them how much they had wounded me. Face down on the floor, I lay sobbing with my head buried in my hands. Suddenly, I gathered myself together for a moment and sat up. I looked over to my right, my eyes swollen from crying, and there it was. It had been there all along but I had never noticed it before--a framed written verse: "The Lord will fight for you; you need only to be still." (Exodus 14:14).

If there was ever a moment where I truly knew the Lord heard me and was speaking to me, it was this moment. God decided to bring it to my attention in my moment of despair and hopelessness when it would have the most significant impact on me.

"*The Lord* will fight for me..." I let the words soak in. I didn't need a man, my church, or even my friends to fight for me. I needed the Lord to fight for me, and though it didn't occur to me until that moment, He already was. I could trust that God would deal with those who hurt me if He wanted to and in His own time. I didn't have to confront them. I cried out for help, He listened, and was showing me that He is my rescuer, ready to rescue me from a life in which I would have always been treading in deep water. He brought me to the shore again where I was always meant to be...where we're all meant to be.

Reflection: How has the Lord revealed Himself to you in a moment of extreme grief or joy? How did it change your perspective on your circumstances? What did you learn?

22nd Sunday in Ordinary Time (Sunday between August 28 and September 3)

All good giving and every perfect gift is from above, coming down from the Father of lights, with whom there is no alteration or shadow caused by change. (James 1:17 NAB-RE)

The Perfect Gift
Dr. Anne Valeri White

I love being a giver of perfect gifts. I could spend hours shopping for special items and assembling combinations of gifts around a theme for birthdays, Christmas, anniversaries, and weddings. The more elaborate the presentation of the gift, the better. I find a special joy in creatively wrapping gifts in beautiful containers, assembling them into baskets with perfect homemade bows, and stacking coordinating boxes from largest to smallest in alternating patterns of gift wrap. I carefully hand-letter cards and gift tags in beautiful script for a flawless finishing touch.

I used to be let down when the receiver of the gift did not marvel at my clever wrapping job before tearing it apart. It took becoming a mother of young children to be able to look past this. My children enthusiastically attack presents, delightfully tossing tissue paper and tearing into gift wrap like mini-tornadoes. They know that the treasure inside is what matters.

Pregnant with my fourth child, I am reminded of how outward appearances can sometimes take the focus away from those perfect gifts. Most days, I am not perfectly put together. My hands and ankles are swollen, I am breathless, my energy is low, and I am physically bursting at the seams. People see and freely comment on my outward fatigue, the gender of my children (all girls), the size of my family, how big or little they think my belly is… you name it! Even strangers ask probing questions such as: "What are you having? Another girl?!? Your poor husband! Are you going to try for a boy? Four kids? You must be crazy! You know how that happens, right?"

When I am not careful, I can let these small trials detract from the joyful anticipation of the tiny, sweet daughter I have yet to meet. I often

121

remind myself that the Father looked at the world, saw what was missing, chose the most perfect gift He could give, then gave my family this very soul I am carrying. His unchanging truth, that every life is precious and meant for a purpose, resounds in my heart.

Reflection: Reflecting on how the Father lavishes us with priceless gifts, describe an instance when outward appearances distracted you from the joy of a treasure in your life. How did you overcome this distraction?

Say to the fearful of heart; Be strong, do not fear! Here is your God, He comes with vindication; With divine recompense He comes to save you. Then the eyes of the blind shall see, and the ears of the deaf be opened; Then the lame shall leap like a stag, and the mute tongue sing for joy.
(Isaiah 35:4-6 NAB)

Radical Obedience
Dr. Anne Valeri White

Katie was a third year medical student on her first clinical experience, and I was tasked with supervising her. To say she was a bundle of anxiety is an understatement. Nothing seemed to be going well for her, and she was having trouble adjusting to her new role. She was a single woman in her early twenties who had recently moved to the area to begin this chapter of her training. In my eyes, her responsibilities were minimal--show up on time, learn as much as she could, put her best foot forward, and study hard. Katie wasn't getting enough sleep, and she always showed up late and disorganized.

Toward the end of her experience, we sat down to review her performance. At the end of our meeting, our conversation turned to her stress level. "The other students and I were talking, and we wonder how you do it," Katie began. "You work full time, take night call, you are about to have your fourth child, and somehow you make it all work. I know this is only going to get harder for me and I am worried that I can't do it. You are so calm. What's your secret?"

Now, I am no model of perfection when it comes to being a working mom. I freely admit that my house is in major disorder and my children ate cereal for tonight's dinner. By some miracle, I have managed to make it to daycare every evening this week before closing. I am organized enough to stay functional, and prioritize a good night's sleep.

My secret is one powerful bit of wisdom from St. Teresa of Calcutta: "God has not called me to be successful; He has called me to be faithful." This faithfulness to my callings as wife, mother, and physician demands radical obedience. Once I got over the fear of losing any sort of personal gain by this obedience, I found the strength to do what others perceive is impossible. This has led to incredible peace.

I do not fear putting my reputation on the line for this obedience anymore, because the graces are so much greater when I fully trust in God's plan for me. For example, I don't spend the precious hours before work and school in leadership meetings. I don't prescribe contraceptives and abortifacients anymore. I don't immerse myself in the time-sink of popular culture just so I can join in the lunchroom banter. These things may make me look foolish to the success-driven secular world, but they have opened my heart to receive true joy.

Reflection: In what areas of your life do you fear radical obedience to God's will? What graces could come from letting go of this fear?

And Jesus went on with his disciples, to the villages of Caesare'a Philippi; and on the way he asked his disciples, "Who do men say that I am?" And they told him, "John the Baptist; and others say, Eli'jah; and others one of the prophets." And he asked them, "But who do you say that I am?" Peter answered him, "You are the Christ." And he charged them to tell no one about him.

And he began to teach them that the Son of man must suffer many things, and be rejected by the elders and the chief priests and the scribes, and be killed, and after three days rise again. And he said this plainly. And Peter took him, and began to rebuke him. But turning and seeing his disciples, he rebuked Peter, and said, "Get behind me, Satan! For you are not on the side of God, but of men."

And he called to him the multitude with his disciples, and said to them, "If any man would come after me, let him deny himself and take up his cross and follow me. For whoever would save his life will lose it; and whoever loses his life for my sake and the gospel's will save it. (Mark 8: 27-35 RSV)

Fill in the Blank
by Josie Valley

When she sat next to me in class, I could tell she was hesitant to tell me what mutual friends had said about me. She thought it might be encouraging, but knew it could potentially be hurtful, too.

"Oh ya! I remember her." "She was always so nice." "But now?! Now she's really into God and stuff. "Isn't she kinda like a Jesus freak or something?"

My friend stopped there. Although those words were meant to be condescending, from the perspective of our mutual friends, she and I knew that they were quite the contrary. You see, I used to be the face of our family business, so and so's girlfriend, a social butterfly, "a nice young woman." Truth is, we are all identified with or find our identity in something or someone. The way we live will either solidify or disprove this association. In Mark, Jesus talked about this with His disciples:

"Who do people say I am?" "Well," they replied, "some say John the Baptist, some say Elijah, and others say you are one of the other prophets." Then he asked them, "But who do you say I am?" Peter replied, "You are the Messiah..."

What if Jesus were to ask you, "(Your Name Here,) who do you say I am?" How would you fill in the blank? How would I? Old me would have answered, "You are Jesus who died for me on the cross and you are my 'Savior.'" And although that is the commendable answer, just saying who He is and what He did was much easier than actually LIVING wholly changed because of it.

At that time of the conversation with my friend, I only had a good understanding of Who He is and what He did, but no deep inward acceptance of why and for whom He did it (me, you). Now, I confidently proclaim, "Jesus, You are my source of life. My redeemer, peace, and my friend. Without you I can do nothing. Lord, You are all I need."

Jesus told His disciples this: '... *"If any of you wants to be my follower, you must give up your own way, take up your cross, and follow me. If you try to hang on to your life, you will lose it. But if you give up your life for my sake and for the sake of the Good News, you will save it.'*

In the first part of this passage, Peter answers who Jesus is to him. Bold and resolute, He states that Jesus is his Messiah. In the next part of the passage Jesus describes what it means to then live this truth out in one's life. Jesus said, "If you give up your life for my sake...you will save it." Little did Peter know that this would pertain to his life quite literally as years later he would die a martyr's death for the cause of Christ. What an example!

What about us? We may not die a martyrs death, but having a martyr's heart is required if we are to truly follow Jesus. Are we willing?

My life doesn't look like it used to, and apparently some have noticed. Although I am still a work in progress, I can say with a boldness like Peter that Jesus is my Messiah, even if it means that I am labeled a Jesus Freak! How will they fill in the blank that best describes you?

May we all be known to live for and love Christ today as audaciously as Peter did back then!

Reflection: Is the way I live directly influenced by who Jesus is to me? Would others recognize a difference in my life because of Jesus? What areas of my life need strengthening so there is no contradiction between what I say and how I live?

For insolent men have risen against me,
  ruthless men seek my life;
  they do not set God before them.
Behold, God is my helper;
  the Lord is the upholder of my life.
He will requite my enemies with evil;
  in thy faithfulness put an end to them.
With a freewill offering I will sacrifice to thee;
  I will give thanks to thy name, O Lord, for it is good.
For thou hast delivered me from every trouble,
  and my eye has looked in triumph on my enemies.
(Psalm 54:3-7 RSV-CE)

Deliver Me, Lord
Rachel Swenson Balducci

When I was a young girl and read about "enemies" in the Bible, my mind often drifted to my favorite book character and her enemy: Laura Ingalls and Nellie Olson. I personally didn't have an enemy like that, but I sure had people in my life who got on my nerves.

I loved the idea of God helping me triumph over them.

Fast forward a few years and I now know the world is filled with people who can, if circumstances allow, get on my nerves. There will always be someone who uses the wrong tone or comes across as rude or unkind, someone who just rubs me the wrong way.

Those people aren't really my enemies -- they are an opportunity for growth. People and circumstances and trials are moments God uses to draw us closer to Him. Throughout a day, there are countless occasions to worry, to fret, to get shaken, and God tells us to Be Not Afraid.

That's the enemy God gives us victory over.

Our enemy is not flesh and blood but is within the spiritual dimension. Our days are filled with circumstances and with people-- neighbors, coworkers, in-laws, even friends--who bother us, but that's not the true enemy. When I'm tempted to feel rejected or annoyed, God

128

has promised to give me victory -- not over the person who has bothered me, but over the wounds that have caused me to feel upset in the first place. What triumph that is!

God will give us victory over the real enemy -- sin and death and the devil himself -- and that is the best promise we can be given.

Reflection: What areas of my life are causing me anxiety? How can I give this to God and allow him to have victory over my "enemy"?

The precepts of the Lord are right,
    rejoicing the heart;
The commandment of the Lord is pure,
    enlightening the eyes;
More to be desired are they than gold,
    even much fine gold;
Sweeter also than honey
    and drippings of the honeycomb.
But who can discern his errors?
    Clear thou me from hidden faults.
Keep back thy servant also from presumptuous sins;
    let them not have dominion over me!
Then I shall be blameless,
    and innocent of great transgression.
Let the words of my mouth and the meditation of my heart
    be acceptable in thy sight,
    O Lord, my rock and my redeemer.
(Psalm 19:8-14 RSV-CE)

The Words of My Mouth
Rachel Swenson Balducci

When I was growing up, my mama had a saying to train us in our speech.

"Before you talk," she would say, "ask yourself: 'Is it true? Is it kind? Is it necessary?'"

As someone who went on to become a newspaper reporter, I gravitated toward the "Is it true?" part, maybe more than I should. As long as I wasn't lying, I told myself, I didn't need to fret.

But of course, in regular conversation, just because something is true doesn't give me the right to share it. That's why the other two parts of the phrase are so important. We speak truth, but only if it's kind. And then, only if it's necessary.

This doesn't always come easy to me. Sometimes I want to share information because it helps explain why a person acts a certain way. Perhaps the "truth" helps a situation make sense. But I have to remember to ask if it's "necessary" to share this information.

I've learned that the best habit is to focus on speaking with kindness and love. The habits of gossip and slander keep us from God because that behavior doesn't build His kingdom. Worse, it actually tears people down. I don't want to have a reputation as someone who walks around saying mean things about people, and this Psalm reminds us how to keep the right focus.

Prayer: Let the words of my heart and the meditations of my mouth be acceptable in your sight, Lord. Let the things I think about and the way I feel line up with your plan for me. Give me freedom Lord, to have a heart so full of love for you that all I can do is sing your praise.

Reflection: Are the words of my mouth and the meditations of my heart acceptable in the sight of God? What areas do I need to clean up? Am I a light to those around me? Do I need to repent of gossip or unkind words?

Blessed are all who fear the Lord, who walk in obedience to Him. You will eat the fruit of your labor; blessings and prosperity will be yours...Yes, this will be the blessing for the man who fears the Lord. May the Lord bless you from Zion; may you see the prosperity of Jerusalem all the days of your life. May you live to see your children's children— peace be on Israel...(Psalm 128:1-6 NIV)

Obedience Brings Blessings
by Judy Nagella

Over the years, I came to a greater understanding of "the fear of the Lord"—walking in obedience to Him. Whenever I heard His voice, I had to first trust, submit, surrender, and act accordingly, then blessings would come!

I love, respect, and revere the Lord; however, walking in obedience is not always easy. When I first learned how to recognize His voice, I questioned many things. He kept calling me out of my comfort zone. Was I hearing Him right? I don't do home parties. I didn't even like going to them when I was invited—why would I want to actually present them? I didn't wear a lot of jewelry...why would I want to sell jewelry? All this sounded crazy! Little did I know the angel pins I sold would minister to so many who were lost.

He also revealed I would be speaking in front of large groups of men and women! "Don't you remember, Lord, how much I hated speech class in high school?"

However, something beautiful happened—I surrendered all to Jesus and began walking in obedience! I trusted that He knew what was best!

In October, 1995, I heard the Lord speak. *"Judy, do you love Me? Feed My sheep."* At the time I had no idea how to feed His sheep, but I knew He would teach me and I chose to follow.

My first assignment from the Lord was to design a prayer devotional; this was the tool, along with my Bible, that allowed me to hear His voice. I continued to sit at the feet of Jesus, writing His messages in my devotional. I walked in obedience by faith, following Him step-by-step. I soon learned how to feed His sheep, and I've been feeding His sheep for 22 years! Yes, at home parties, selling jewelry—angel pins, and other inspirational items; AND...speaking in front of small and large groups of men and women!

The enemy's plan has been for me to grow weary and lose my heart to follow the Lord. I often felt exhausted during the many storms I faced, but I continued to obey. If it weren't for my prayer devotional, I probably would have quit years ago and missed countless blessings.

I thank God for giving me the perseverance to always write in my devotional. I often went back to it to confirm His leading. Many times, He reminded me, *"Judy, do not become weary in doing well; for in due season you shall reap, if you do not lose heart and do not quit"* (Galatians 6:9).

My focus had to remain on not giving up, but standing steadfast in my walk with the Lord. In due season [in God's divine timing] I would reap His awesome blessings.

I finally grasped the Lord's objective in my life...when I felt discouraged and lost my focus, I was no longer walking in obedience to Him and I lost my joy! Today, choose obedience—Choose JOY and receive your blessings!

Reflection: Was there a time in your life when you "chose" to walk in obedience to the Lord's leading? Write about the blessing you received because of the choice you made.

Teach us to number our days aright, that we may gain a heart of wisdom. Relent, O Lord! How long will it be? Have compassion on your servants. Satisfy us in the morning with your unfailing love, that we may sing for joy and be glad all our days. Make us glad for as many days as you have afflicted us, for as many years as we have seen trouble. May your deeds be shown to your servants, your splendor to their children. May the favor of the Lord our God rest upon us; establish the work of our hands for us—yes, establish the work of our hands. (Ps. 90:12-17 NIV)

When Life Throws You a Curve Ball
by Robin Swoboda

In April of 2016, I got the diagnosis that one in eight women will get and that no one wants to hear. "You have breast cancer."

In the months prior to my diagnosis, I had been sensing God's presence in a more real and tangible way than I ever had in my life.

You see, I have lived a pretty trouble-free life. My mother always said that things just came too easy for me. That began to change in 2011 with the ending of my 20-year marriage.

Since then, I rebounded and married the first guy who came along, for what was a very turbulent and abusive 4 years. My mom has died, so has my baby brother. I was in an accident on a horse which broke my leg. And I had to put down my little dog, Lulu, who was only three-and-a-half years old when encephalitis caused her little five-pound body so much discomfort I had to do the humane thing.

Yet through it all, I have remained joyful. Oh I have cried ugly cries that left my eyes red and swollen. I have cried out to God and asked "Why?"

But with each passing affliction, I sensed it was not an obstacle but an opportunity from God Himself to experience His grace and mercy. With each affliction, He is molding me for eternity.

My days on this earth are numbered and dwindling but they are sweeter now. I am not living an easy life anymore, but I am living a life filled with God's unfailing love…and there is nothing sweeter than that.

Reflection: Knowing that not one thing happens to us without God's permission, what obstacle or affliction can you turn into an opportunity to see God's unfailing love and sing for joy because He is molding you for eternity? Write a prayer below, asking Him to help you see the opportunity in this trial.

And James and John, the sons of Zeb'edee, came forward to him, and said to him, "Teacher, we want you to do for us whatever we ask of you." And he said to them, "What do you want me to do for you?" And they said to him, "Grant us to sit, one at your right hand and one at your left, in your glory." But Jesus said to them, "You do not know what you are asking. Are you able to drink the cup that I drink, or to be baptized with the baptism with which I am baptized?" And they said to him, "We are able." And Jesus said to them, "The cup that I drink you will drink; and with the baptism with which I am baptized, you will be baptized; but to sit at my right hand or at my left is not mine to grant, but it is for those for whom it has been prepared." And when the ten heard it, they began to be indignant at James and John. And Jesus called them to him and said to them, "You know that those who are supposed to rule over the Gentiles lord it over them, and their great men exercise authority over them. But it shall not be so among you; but whoever would be great among you must be your servant, and whoever would be first among you must be slave of all. For the Son of man also came not to be served but to serve, and to give his life as a ransom for many." (Mark 10:35-45 RSV)

Sibling Rivalry
by Katherine L. Szerdy

My sister Linda is a prayer warrior—a woman who spends a lot of time on her knees in her prayer closet or wherever God calls her to pray. First thing in the morning seven days a week 365 days a year, she starts her day in the Word and in prayer—sometimes for hours—not in a legalistic way but as a natural response to the call of the Holy Spirit to make her relationship with her heavenly Father first and foremost. She is the one person my own children ask me to call for prayerful support when facing trials. I've never known anyone quite like her! She has received remarkable answers to prayer including healings of low self-esteem, anxiety, depression, relationships, finances, and illnesses! The answers she has received to prayer could literally fill volumes of prayer journals!

As a young girl, I felt close to God and was thrilled to receive a Bible for memorizing Psalm 100 in third grade Sunday School. Through my teen years and early twenties, I would open the Good Book first thing in the morning, seeking a closer relationship with Him and carry it with me to school to read whenever I had a few minutes. A number of years later, I pursued a graduate degree in liberal studies with a concentration in religious studies and took several theology and biblical history courses thinking all that academic knowledge would get me closer to the Lord. I even completed a Master's Thesis entitled, *The History of Heaven, Hell, and Purgatory from Antiquity through the Middle Ages*. Yet, I struggled to understand His love for me. I didn't have much time to spend in the Word first thing in the morning, but spent an abundance of hours at the campus library filling my head with knowledge about Him.

My sister is five years younger than me, but she is years ahead in spiritual wisdom. She didn't start out that way, however. [I share this story with her permission.] Linda barely squeaked through high school and never went to college. As a young wife and mother, she suffered from addictions, fears, and feelings of inadequacy until one day, she felt she had nowhere else to turn. She knelt down and surrendered her life to Jesus. Hers was truly a conversion and all those who knew her recognized that something was different about her.

As in the example in Mark 10, we see that even the disciples experienced jealousy toward each other in vying for a place next to Jesus. I'm ashamed to admit that as I watched my sister blossom in her faith walk, I coveted the transforming power of the Holy Spirit I saw at work in her life. Eventually, I came to understand that no matter how much formal education one has or what church one belongs to or how many church committees on which one sits has not much to do with spiritual growth--we grow not by knowledge but by wisdom, and that wisdom is gleaned mainly through daily due diligence—time spent with Him, one on one, in the closet of our homes or our hearts "drinking from the cup that he drinks"—and making that time an absolute priority.

Reflection: When in your life have you felt closest to the Lord? What spiritual disciplines were you practicing at the time which enabled you to draw nigh to Him?

...On hearing that it was Jesus of Nazareth, he began to cry out and say, "Jesus, son of David, have pity on me." And many rebuked him, telling him to be silent, But he kept calling out all the more... Jesus told him, "Go your way; your faith has saved you."... (Mk. 10:46-52 NAB)

Pray without Ceasing
by Janie Reinart

On the wall of my office, I have word art that says, "Pray without ceasing." When I pray for special intentions, I light a candle in my home to help me focus and pray all day long. I am persistent in praying for my family and friends.

When my son deployed with the 216th Engineer Battalion, I put on a lapel pin—the kind that holds a small picture in a frame—a picture of my soldier boy in his National Guard uniform. I wore my son's picture over my heart every day. Because of that picture, strangers stopped me around town, at the store, at church and asked, "Is that your son?"

I answered proudly, "Yes, please pray for him and for the safety of all our soldiers." No one ever refused my request.

My pastor, always says, "When you don't know what to do—pray."

To stay strong spiritually, on March 19th, the feast of Saint Joseph, I made the commitment to go to mass every day and become a prayer warrior. I continually realized how much I needed God. At one point my son emailed me: *"–I am strong because you are strong."* We were strong for each other.

By the grace of God, we made it through the fifteen months my son was away from home. He narrowly escaped death several times. Now all that was left was the 600-mile convoy back to Kuwait. Our soldiers are most vulnerable on a convoy. Remembering what my pastor said, I asked if we could have a three-day prayer vigil (the same days the 216th was on the road).

I signed people up to pray every hour for three days and nights. We started the first night at nine pm in the chapel (5 am in Iraq) and stayed all night finishing up the first day with mass at 9 am in the morning.

Every time I thought I could not possibly stay awake any longer, someone new came to pray with me. These angels continued praying around the clock for the next two days at home. As it turned out, my son was bumped from the convoy and got to fly out on the airstrip.

When my son got to Kuwait his sergeant on the convoy said, " I can't believe we had no delays, no breakdowns, and no attacks!" My son just smiled and said, "You had a lot of people praying for you."

My son said he felt closer to God during his deployment then at any other time of his life. By the grace of God our prayers made us strong. I was changed and humbled knowing our soldiers sacrifice so much for us each day. I was changed and humbled by all those who prayed with me.

Reflection: When were you humbled by an answer to prayer? Write about a time you brought your needs to God.

31st Sunday in Ordinary Time (Sunday between October 30 and November 5)

The Lord our God is Lord alone! You shall love the Lord your God with all your heart, with all your soul, with all your mind, and with all your strength . (Mark 12:30 NAB)

Loving the Jones's
by Brooke Taylor

When I was a young single woman, I chased ideals about what the perfect life, perfect family, perfect career should look like. Not grounded in my faith, I was easily rattled by things beyond my control. I struggled with anxiety. I exerted a great deal of energy attempting to chase the picture of perfection I held in my mind. I remember discovering a book in the Christian self-help section of our local bookstore called *Be Anxious for Nothing* by Joyce Meyer. Because of my insecurities at the time, the subtitle grabbed me --"The Art of Casting Your Cares and Resting in God." At a time when I was grabbing ahold of anything and everything that would bring me happiness, reading this book began to point me in the right direction. As St. Augustine said and I was beginning to learn, "Our hearts are restless, O Lord, until they rest in thee."

A few years later, my husband joined RCIA,[1] for which I served as his sponsor, and I began to thirst for the truths of Christ, desiring to draw closer to Him as never before. At the same time, I started training for a half marathon. I often jogged through an upper class neighborhood with large, sprawling homes. When I first began my training, my thoughts were filled with envy for those who occupied the beautiful houses. I would grumble, "I bet they are all in debt." I assumed the money didn't come honestly, or the parents worked so much that they never spent time with their children. In short, I had developed a jealous, bitter spirit.

Months later, providentially, my half marathon training came to a close around the same time RCIA came to completion. By this time, I

---

[1] The nine-month process for joining my faith tradition.

noticed a complete transformation of heart. No longer jealous about what I didn't have, I praised God for prosperity in the lives of my neighbors and asked the Lord to bless the souls inside the big homes. My jealousy over the Joneses grew into a sincere joy for Jehovah-Jireh, God provider. It was a radical change of spirit and I loved how it felt—I was free of the restlessness and resentment that came from my believing that what the Lord had given me was not enough. So many of the self-imposed pressures I had placed on myself began to feel petty, insignificant and superficial. And they were!

It's not to say that I haven't again struggled with comparing myself to others, coveting or feeling "less than." But the truths I learned during that season of my life have served me well. I am no longer concerned about trying to compete with younger moms, prettier moms, wealthier friends. I celebrate their gifts as I recognize that God has entrusted me with my own. My job is to use my gifts for His glory. There is a freedom in that. There is freedom in knowing that I am not tethered to this face, my skin, my weight, or the size of my home. Those things are not the source of my peace. God's gaze is always fixed upon us, like a loving parent. It is *we* who turn away. By following God's call to love Him above all else, we turn our faces back to Him and discover the Source of peace.

Reflection: Can you recall a time in your life when your love for God gave you "new eyes" to see a situation? What book, podcast, sermon, or friend has God used to help you see with "new eyes"? How can you live out the commandment to love God with all of your heart today?

The Lord sets the prisoners free;
 the Lord opens the eyes of the blind.
The Lord lifts up those who are bowed down;
  the Lord loves the righteous.
The Lord watches over the strangers;
  he upholds the orphan and the widow,
  but the way of the wicked he brings to ruin.
The Lord will reign forever,
  your God, O Zion, for all generations.
Praise the Lord! (*Psalm 146:7-10 NRSV*)

She Shuddered
by Joan Spieth

Every one of us experiences hurt, pain and grief. Being born the caboose of a large family, I end up being the last one standing. As of this day, my parents, five of my sisters and two of my four brothers, as well as others, have been called from this life.

When my own husband was diagnosed with cancer a few years ago, we entered into a sacred and searing journey. That journey continues even five years after his death.

Our Blessed Mother became an even greater role model as a widow and as a silent sentry at the foot of the cross. An Easter morning inspiration has given me comfort and peace:

> *She shuddered.*
> *She was so cold. It was as if in the holding the lifeless body of*
> *her son the coldness of death*
> *had attached itself to her own body.*
> *Her mind nor her eyes could focus save only*
> *on the name of her son.*
> *She was spent, drained. Her eyes were closed and her body was*
> *almost involuntarily rocking. She had rocked him in her arms*
> *when he was a baby and she rocked his dead body when*
> *he was released from the cross.*

Then a warmth started to come into her toes, her feet and rise through her whole body. Her hands stopped trembling. She felt like a warm lamb's blanket was being wrapped around her. Her room was becoming brighter and all of her senses surged to full awareness.

Her faith and her mother's heart beheld her Son.
The sweet fullness of reunion!
There were no tears – just torrents of thanksgiving.
She could feel his beating heart under her cheek.
Then she heard his voice say, "Mother."

Reflection: When you were going through a rough time, how has God comforted you in a personal way?

The Lord is the portion of my inheritance and my cup;
You support my lot.
The lines have fallen to me in pleasant places;
Indeed, my heritage is beautiful to me.
I will bless the Lord who has counseled me;
Indeed, my mind instructs me in the night.
I have set the Lord continually before me;
Because He is at my right hand, I will not be shaken.
Therefore my heart is glad and my glory rejoices;
My flesh also will dwell securely.
For You will not abandon my soul to Sheol;
Nor will You ⌊allow Your ⌊Holy One to ⌊undergo decay.
You will make known to me the path of life;
In Your presence is fullness of joy;
In Your right hand there are pleasures forever. (Psalm 16:5-11 NASB)

Praise Him Anyhow!
by Pastor Linda C. Isaiah

In 1991 I was severely depressed. I was attending church regularly, reading my Bible, teaching a Sunday school class, supervising a booming nursery ministry and working with a husband. As you can see, I hid my emotions well. My depression stemmed from my father's unexpected death, at least I thought so at the time. Don't get me wrong, we didn't have a good father-daughter relationship. After my Dad's death, I had no one to blame for my pain. All of my past came tumbling down all around me. I was around 30 or so and felt like I was losing my mind. I cried out to God! I recognized that I needed professional help.

With much fear I started seeing a counselor once a week. I had so much stuff to uncover that my counselling extended for over five years. Yep, exactly. I asked God why me? Why did I have to suffer so much?

During that more than five year journey, I voluntarily admitted myself into an inpatient unit (the proper term is Psych Hospital) for fourteen days. During this hospitalization, I experienced a dark night of the soul. Here I searched for God and He gave me my portion, Psalm 16:5, and my cup. He assured me that he had me in the palm of his hands, that He had a specific purpose for my life.

Even at night when I heard others screaming and crying, I could trust God with my heart. He reminded me that I was safe in his arms (Psalm 16:7-8).

In my deep despair and emptying out, my faith was not shaken and I began to praise the Lord for all of his goodness toward me even in a Psych Hospital. As I poured more junk out of me, he was filling me with His Holy Spirit and praise. God assured me that I would live and not die!!! Even when it felt like death, it became a glorious light. I can tell you this--my God can deliver you from death to life. He is my deliverer, my rock, my fortress, my redeemer, my friend, my elder brother, my strength, my hope, my joy, my all in all. I will yet praise Him. Hallelujah!!

Reflection: Can you recall a time in your life when you lost your joy? Write down when and how God brought you through the darkness into His glorious light. If you are struggling now, read Pastor Linda's devotion each day this week for a daily dose of encouragement. Let the words soak in. Then turn to Him in prayer and trust that He will deliver you!

*Pilate entered the praetorium again and called Jesus, and said to him,
"Are you the King of the Jews?"*

*Jesus answered, "Do you say this of your own accord, or did others
say it to you about me?"*

*Pilate answered, "Am I a Jew? Your own nation and the chief priests
have handed you over to me; what have you done?"*

*Jesus answered, "My kingship is not of this world; if my kingship were
of this world, my servants would fight, that I might not be handed over to
the Jews; but my kingship is not from the world."*

*Pilate said to him, "So you are a king?" Jesus answered, "You say
that I am a king. For this I was born, and for this I have come into the
world, to bear witness to the truth. Every one who is of the truth hears
my voice."* (John 18: 33-37 RSV-CE)

Kingship on the Cross
by Fr. Nathan Cromly

Despite what many people might say, I remain convinced that most
people today are trying to do good. And yet, despite our best efforts, evil
and suffering abound and even seem to increase. Suffering (in its many
forms) creeps into our life on a daily basis, and we seem powerless to
stop it. In the light of the intense realities of evil and pain, what does it
mean to say that Christ is the King of our Universe?

The Gospel gives us the key to understanding what this means. In
today's Gospel, Christ reveals to Pilate that His kingship is of a spiritual
nature, not a worldly one. Remember, Christ is not finally declared to be
the "King of the Jews" until He is hung upon the Cross.

This is important. On the Cross, Christ "draws all men to Himself,"
claiming all souls for His Father in Heaven. His blood and His act of
redemption reveal God's unique love for each person, and His desire for
each person to participate in the heavenly kingdom. In Christ crucified,
our suffering and the trials of our fallen world become a song of
victory. Love triumphs through the wood.

On the Cross, Christ's love triumphs over evil and death. Though they remain part of our experience, they are transformed. They are claimed by Him and redeemed as messengers of a greater Love. Jesus reigns, even in a broken world! He reigns through this world's brokenness by redeeming it and transforming it.

Following the King in trust does not mean that evil and suffering will make sense to us now. One example of meeting suffering with trust is the Dutch Christian Corrie ten Boom, who was imprisoned during World War II in German prison camps, where she watched several of her family members die. She often quoted a poem called "The Weaver," which envisions life as a weaving project crafted by God. The poem concludes:

> *Not till the looms are silent and the shuttles cease to fly,*
> *Will God unroll the canvas and explain the reason why*
> *The dark threads are as needful in the Weaver's skillful hand*
> *As the threads of gold and silver in the pattern He has planned.*

It is an amazing thought: The King of the Universe does not ignore the threads of brokenness and pain that weave through our life, but incorporates them into His masterful plan. He takes it upon Himself, drawing us closer to Him by the brokenness and inviting us to be sharers in His kingdom.

"For this I came into the world," Christ says to Pilate, and to us, "to testify to the truth." The truth that Christ the King bears witness to is that God is Love. Trusting in His words, let us offer our suffering to Him, that it may be absorbed into the King of the Universe's merciful design of love.

Reflection: What brokenness can you offer Christ, the King of the Universe, to carry in love to the Father?

Choose Joy

by Josie Valley

It was not for riches or fame
No agenda or platform to claim
Nor was there a motive that they then could see
The *joy* before Him was You and Me.

He was fully aware upon arrival
Of the agony that would be His fate
Forward He walked without hesitation
For His *joy* He chose this date.

He would experience excruciating separation
From His Father's perfect love
Coming to a home that was never His
For His *joy*, He left His throne above.

With each blow to His back
His body buckled to the pain
When nails pierced His hands
It was for His *joy*, His gain.

Although He knew many would deny His love
And think His a story of the past
He walked the road to Calvary
Knowing His *joy* could be with Him at last.

With each gasping breath on the Cross
Leading to the whispered plea of despair
It mattered not what was before Him
It was love for His *joy* that truly kept Him there.

When Scripture says, 'for the *joy* set before Him'
He endured the cross
This '*joy*' refers to all mankind
He intended that none would be lost

If we can accept that we are His *joy*
And allow our hearts to believe

We can live here well and loved
Because His peace we will receive

He chose the *joy* set before Him
Knowing pain would be His plight
Choosing joy is never easy
When heartache is within sight,

But when we know that we are loved
And believe He chose the likes of you and me
We can walk through pain more confident
Because of the promises He made upon that tree.

When He promised it was finished
He meant He did all that needed to be done
So that we would never know one day here
Without help from the Holy One.

In choosing *joy* He made a promise
His Holy Spirit would remain
Amongst those who believe Him for this gift
A way to alleviate the world's pressures and pain.

We can choose joy today and share it
Because of the one who chose us first
We can be a light in the darkness
And offer His love to those who thirst.

For You are His *JOY*, Friend
So rest assured in your mind
Everything He did was to prove
No greater love you will ever find!

He chose to suffer so that we didn't have to!

"For the joy set before him he endured the cross, scorning its shame, and sat down at the right hand of the throne of God." Hebrews 12:2b

About the Author

Brooke Taylor, a wife and mother of five, is a radio personality, speaker, and writer. After ten years as morning show co-host for a prominent Christian radio station, Brooke left her full time position to care for her family.

Brooke is a popular host and speaker at events all over the United States including Bloggy Con, the National Ms. Wheelchair U.S.A. Pageant, Catholic Conferences for Women, and she has appeared on EWTN.

Currently, she hosts the popular podcast "Good Things Radio."

Brooke has interviewed film stars and Christian recording artists, politicians and pastors such as former Speaker of the House Newt Gingrich, Dr. James Dobson, Franklin Graham, Raymond Arroyo, Christopher West, TobyMac, Nicole C. Mullen, Dolly Parton, to name a few.

She has also traveled to Guatemala and Haiti to raise awareness and funds with the ministry Food for the Poor . You can find out more about Brooke by visiting www.BrookeTaylor.Us

---

Never let anything so fill you with sorrow as to make you forget the joy of the Risen Christ. We all long for Heaven where God is, but we have it in our power to be in Heaven with him right now to be happy with him at this very moment. But being happy with him now means:

- loving as he loves
- helping as he helps;
- giving as he gives
- serving as he serves
- rescuing as he rescues
- being with him 24 hours a day
- touching him in his distressing disguise
- in the poor and suffering

--Saint Mother Teresa of Calcutta

Biographies of our Contributors

Rachel Balducci is a writer and speaker. She is a co-host of The Gist on CatholicTV and a columnist for *The Southern Cross* for the Diocese of Savannah. Her next book, *Order Brings Peace*, comes out Fall 2018.

Trish Berg is an author, speaker, and professor. Her four books include *A Scrapbook of Christmas Firsts* and *The Great American Supper Swap*. At forty-five, she earned her doctorate and she currently teaches management at Walsh University. She and her husband, Mike, are now launching four teens and young adults into college and life and preparing for the joy of the empty nest.

Anna Bertram is a Catholic wife and mom to two children here on Earth and one saint in heaven, whom she briefly knew for eight months. She co-leads a Catholic mothers group, serves as a PSR Catechist and a music minister in the Praise and Worship Team at St. John Neumann. You can follow her on Instagram at withamothersheart.

Jeff Cavins is the founder of the Great Adventure Bible Study System at Ascension Press. He is an author of many books and speaks about Scripture around the world. He is married to his wife, Emily and has three daughters.

Leah Cheng lives in North Canton, Ohio, where she home schools her three sons and prays for her husband who is stationed overseas. She spends much of her spare time reading and baking. The peaceful time between the boys' bedtime and hers is spent in prayer and she'd rather call September early fall instead of late summer.

Ruth Clifford is a wife to David and stay-at-home mom of three beautiful boys: Emmanuel, Gabriel, and Elijah. She is passionate about God, her family, and ice cream.

Father Nathan Cromly, CSJ, is a Catholic priest of the Congregation of St. John. His efforts in the New Evangelization include preaching, teaching, and founding Eagle Eye Ministries, through which he leads young people on backpacking trips to places like Scotland, Iceland, Hawaii, and Alaska. Most recently, Fr. Nathan has devoted his energy to establishing the Saint John Institute, a fully-accredited MBA program designed to form and equip evangelizers for the modern world.

Jenni Ellis' first priority is her relationship with God. She is blessed to be the mother of an eight-year-old son. After 30 years in Atlanta, she has found herself back in Richmond, Virginia, as the principal at St. Mary's Catholic School. Her favorite verse is 1 Thessalonians 5:16-18: "Be cheerful no matter what; pray all the time; thank God no matter what happens."

Michele Faehnle is a wife, mother of four, school nurse, author and speaker. In her free time she enjoys volunteering for the church as the co-chair of the Columbus Catholic Women's Conference. She is the co-author of two publications: *The Friendship Project: The Catholic Woman's Guide to Making and Keeping Fabulous Faith Filled Friends* and *Divine Mercy For Moms: Sharing the Lessons of St. Faustina* through Ave Maria Press. You can find more of her writing at divinemercyformoms.com and www.thefriendshipprojectbook.com.

Jen Gerber is a wife and homeschooling mother of five on Earth and one in Heaven. She and her husband Chad converted to Catholicism from the Mennonite faith in 2008 after living in Oxford England, where Chad pursued his doctoral studies in theology. They live on a homestead in the heart of Ohio's Amish country.

Lisa M. Hendey is the author of The Grace of Yes and the Chime Travelers series of children's fiction. The founder of CatholicMom.com,

Lisa travels internationally, writing and speaking on faith and service. Visit her at www.LisaHendey.com.

Pastor Linda C. Isaiah dispenses the 'Spirit of Hope" everywhere she goes. She helps women navigate the tough stuff of life, through the practicality of The Word of God. Her unique ability to use humor brings healing to the hearts of hurting women. Linda teaches women how to fight by faith for all God Has for them!

Emily Jaminet is a wife and mother of seven children. She is active in her community in Columbus, Ohio. She co-authored *Divine Mercy for Moms* and *The Friendship Project*. She enjoys speaking, blogging at www.CatholicMom.com and sharing with others her love for Christ!

Melody Lyons is a Jesus loving homeschooling mother of eight who is also an author, chronic illness survivor and thriver, speaker, business owner, dreamer, and happy wife. She writes about healing and how to live a free, faithful, joyful, healthy life at her website: www.theessentialmother.com

Angela Miller is a Catholic wife, homeschooling mom, clinical psychologist, and science enthusiast. In her elusive free time, she loves to read and collect fancy pieces of paper from institutions of higher learning. She lives in Canton, Ohio, with her exceedingly patient and supportive husband and their four young children.

Marie Monsour is a wife and mother to 10 children, ranging in age from 24 down to 7 (Hmm 24/7 sounds familiar). When she is not filling out forms (which she does for a living), she can be found spending time with her husband and children and laughing at the days to come. Marie and Dave and their family reside in Northeast Ohio.

Judy Nagella is simply a handmaid of the Lord, filled with the Holy Spirit who loves to "touch hearts and transform lives for Jesus!" She is the Founder/President of "Seeds Of Joy," a ministry in Ravenna,

Ohio. Judy encourages others as an Inspirational Speaker, Teacher, Evangelist, Writer, and Praise Performer.

Vicki Przybylski is a police officer who is married to her hero Nik, also a police officer. They have three beautiful children, Amelia [married to Matt], Drake and Aiden. She enjoys volunteering for youth group, PTU, and Girl Scouts. She is a proud member of the Arise retreat team and enjoys reading in her free time.

Janie Reinart wears many hats--educator, author, professional puppeteer, and interactive musical storyteller, gentle clown, poet-in-residence, and blogger. Best of all, Janie loves playing with words and writing for children. She lives in Ohio with her husband. She's always up for a game, bubbles, or dress-up. Ask her fourteen (almost fifteen) grandchildren.

Betty Schnitzler is a Catholic wife, married to Greg for 36 years, mother of three adopted children, one son-in-law and grandmother of 5-year-old Eleanor. She is retired and blessed to be able to help take care of Eleanor after school. She is passionate about pro-life issues and enjoys spending time with her Sisters-in-Christ from her parish and other Catholic groups.

Rachel G. Scott is the wife of Willie Scott Jr., a mother of 7, speaker, author, and mentor. She received her Bachelor's Degree from Kansas State University and her Master's Degree from The University of Mary. She has written several books to encourage and support Blended families and is deeply devoted to God, her husband, and her children. Learn more about Rachel at www.betterthanblended.com

Joan Mary Spieth is a native of Sandusky, Ohio. Her childhood dream was to become a Sister of Notre Dame. In August of 1962, she became Sister Mary Josena. A health issue detoured her and several years later, she married. She and her husband, Larry, were blessed to have three children and a marriage of 44 years. Cancer took his life in 2012. She is presently active in parish life and serves as Chair of Magnificat in Stark County, Ohio. (And she is Brooke's Mom!)

Robin Swoboda is a Cleveland icon best known for her career in television and radio, and yes, even as a film actress. Although Robin is currently a co-host of the weekly show, "Retirement Solutions with Bill Smith," she is far from retired. She serves as a popular columnist at the Akron Beacon Journal as well as a speaker and host for public and church events! Her favorite quote is: "Sometimes, on the way to a dream, you get lost and find a better one."

A recent Catholic convert and published poet, **Katherine L. Szerdy** spent twenty years helping elementary, middle and high school students discover their "author within." Recently retired, she looks forward to concentrating on her own writing—she is currently working on a women's devotional, a book on surviving menopause and four children's books!

Ali Towle lives in Madison, Wisconsin, with her graduate student husband and fluffy Siberian cat. When she is not painting, she is a nanny to two incredible little girls. Ali is a self-taught artist with a B.A. degree in Religious Studies from the University of Wisconsin at Stevens Point. You can find her work at her Etsy shop, Saint Script.

Joy Trachsel is a blogger, author, advocate for the unborn and international speaker for women's events. She can be heard on Moody Radio Cleveland as part of the Pause for prayer team. She is passionate about women saying Yes to God. Get to know Joy better by visiting www.joytrachsel.com.

Taylor Tripodi is a 23-year-old native of Cleveland, Ohio. A recent graduate of Franciscan University, she received her degrees in Theology and Catechetics. She absolutely loves being a Youth Minister and using her gifts of music to accompany her in ministry to people all across the country. Being the oldest of nine children and being a part of a big, Italian family are a few of her greatest joys in life. In her spare time, she enjoys hiking outdoors, getting caught in the rain, singing and writing music, traveling, finding the perfect scented candle, and attempting to speak with different accents.

An Ohio native, **Lori Triplett** is a Christian singer/songwriter, pianist, and worship leader based in Nashville, TN. Her music is written from the perspective of her Christian faith and addresses the human experience through that lens. You can learn more about Lori and her music by visiting www.loritriplett.com.

Josie Valley is the founder of Minutes Matter, a faith-filled online ministry that helps women live intentionally, discover their unique purpose, and link arms with other women. She is a writer, speaker, and counselor, but is most satisfied in being wife and mama. She'd love to connect with you! www.josievalley.com

Tanya Weitzel lives with her husband and son in Connecticut. She is a wife, mom, homemaker, homeschool teacher, library assistant, and writer. She blogs at Startingfromscratcheveryday.com, guest writes on www.Catholicmom.com, and contributed to *The Catholic Mom's Prayer Companion*. She enjoys walking, reading, and a good cup of coffee.

Dr. Anne Valeri White is a working mom of four and a Catholic family physician. She has been married to her husband Mark since 2004. Anne is on the Arise Retreat team, enjoys writing, cooking, teaching residents and medical students, and delivering babies.

Acknowledgments

To the Arise retreat team: Anne, Angela, Betty, Christina, Marie, Vicki and Fr. Nathan Cromly, CSJ, thank you for believing in this ministry.

To the Editor and Project Manager, Katherine Szerdy, this book would not be possible without your faithful "Fiat."

Thank you to all the writers who lent their voices to this project. Thank you for allowing us into your hearts by sharing your stories. You are an inspiration and a light.

To my husband and children, thank you for your unconditional love and motivation.

> A joyful heart
> is the normal result of
> a heart burning with love.
> It is the gift of the Spirit,
> a share in the joy of Jesus,
> living in the soul.
>
> *--Saint Mother Teresa of Calcutta*